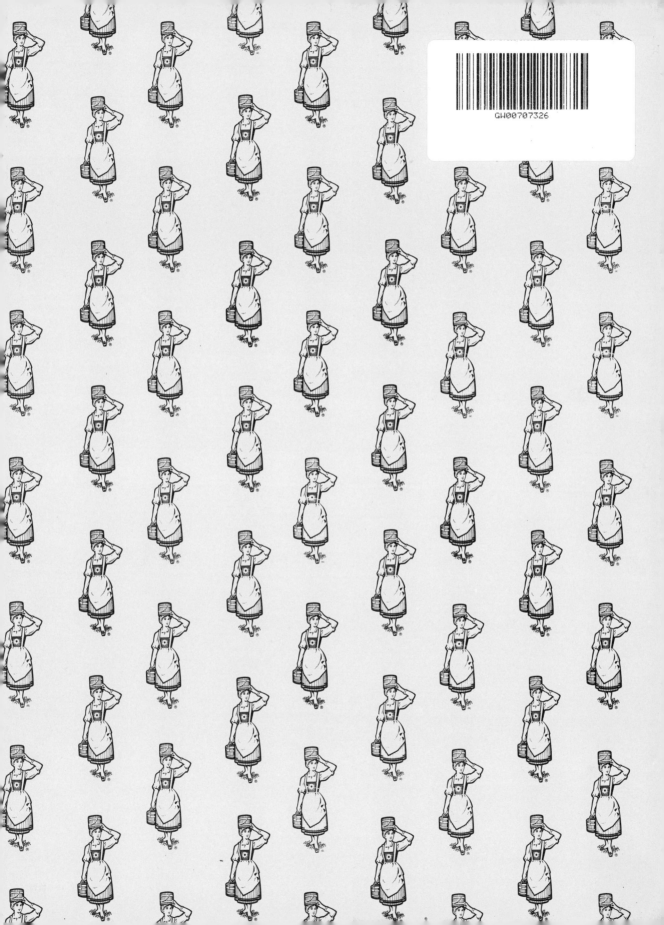

Nayan Ravaliya

Milkmaid®

Gold Collection

OF 101 DESSERTS

 **UBSPD**

UBS Publishers' Distributors Ltd.

New Delhi Bombay Bangalore Madras
Calcutta Patna Kanpur London

© Copyright Nestlé
First Edition 1991
Second Edition 1992

ISBN 81-85273-50-2

UBS Publishers' Distributors Ltd.
5 Ansari Road, New Delhi 110 002

Designed by Tara Sinha Associates.
Photography by Pradeep Das Gupta

Printed by Toppan Printing Co. (S) Ltd., Singapore

CONTENTS

F O R E W O R D

Mmm Milkmaid ! You can do wonders with it!

Housewives in India and abroad have been cooking up delicious
desserts quickly and conveniently with Milkmaid. Much to the
delight of their families and friends.

Sometimes they have used their own recipes. Sometimes Nestlé
recipes. In India we have, since we started in 1984, already
distributed over $1\frac{1}{2}$ million Milkmaid Recipe Booklets. These are
given to all consumers who ask for them. And still almost 10,000
requests keep coming in every month.

Many of these consumers have suggested that we publish a larger
collection of recipes for Milkmaid desserts. We are thankful to
them for sowing the seeds of the idea and to all Milkmaid
consumers who have written to us, for providing the
encouragement to develop the *Milkmaid Gold Collection of 101
Desserts*.

We are sure you will enjoy making the desserts for your family and
friends just as much as we enjoyed creating the book for you.

Bon Appetit!

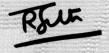

Traditional Favourites

Kheer

❦

Gajar Ka Halwa

❦

Phirni

❦

Amras

❦

Amrakhand

❦

Seviyan

❦

Malai Jamun

❦

Kesari Bhaat

Kheer

Preparation Time : 5 minutes

Cooking Time : 20-25 minutes

To serve 8

Ingredients

Milkmaid : 1 tin
Rice : 100 gm
Milk : 1 litre
Chopped nuts
Elaichi powder } (optional)

Method

1. Wash rice and pressure cook in milk for 10 minutes (or cook on slow fire, till rice is soft).

2. Add Milkmaid and cook for another 5 to 7 minutes, stirring constantly, until the *kheer* reaches the desired consistency.

3. Remove from fire.

4. Serve garnished with nuts/*elaichi* powder.

Quick Tip

If kheer is served chilled, keep it a little sweeter because cold kheer tastes less sweet than hot kheer.

Kheer

Gajar Ka Halwa

Gajar Ka Halwa

Preparation Time : 10-15 minutes

Cooking Time : 45-50 minutes

To serve 10

Ingredients

Milkmaid : 1 tin
Milk : 5 cups
Carrots : $^3/_4$ kg
Sugar (to taste) : 1-2 tbsp
Ghee : 2 tsp
Nuts/Raisins : 50 gm (optional)

Method

1. Grate carrots. Add to milk and bring to a boil. Cook on slow fire, stirring occasionally till milk dries up.

2. Add Milkmaid and sugar. Cook on a slow fire till dry (about 25 to 30 minutes) stirring occasionally.

3. Add *ghee* and cook for another 10 minutes.

4. Garnish with nuts, raisins and serve hot.

10

Phirni

Preparation Time : 30-40 minutes

Cooking Time : 10-15 minutes

To serve 8

Ingredients

Milkmaid : 1 tin
Milk : 3 cups
Rice : 100 gm
Elaichi : 2-3, powdered
Rose water : 1 tsp
Rose petals : few

Method

1. Soak rice in water for 30 minutes to 1 hour. Drain water and grind to a fine paste.

2. Add milk to paste and heat together, stirring constantly so that the mixture does not stick to the bottom. Bring to a boil. Cook for 5 to 7 minutes. Add Milkmaid and remove from fire.

3. Add *elaichi* powder and rose water. Leave to cool and set in a refrigerator.

4. Serve garnished with rose petals.

Phirni

Amras

Preparation Time : 10 minutes

No cooking required

To serve 6

Ingredients

Milkmaid : $^1/_2$ tin
Mangoes : 3 (medium size)
Milk : 1 cup

Method

1. Peel mangoes and remove pulp.

2. Mash the pulp well with hand or blend coarsely.

3. Add Milkmaid and cold milk. Chill.

4. Serve well chilled.

Quick Tip

In case mangoes are fibrous, pass amras through a sieve before serving.

Amrakhand

Preparation Time : 15 minutes

No cooking required

To serve 8

Ingredients

Milkmaid : $^1/_2$ tin
Curd : $^1/_2$ kg
Paneer : 100 gm
Mango essence : 1 tsp

Method

1. Put curd in a muslin cloth and allow to hang for 10 minutes. Press to make sure that excess water is removed.

2. Mash *paneer* till smooth and creamy. Blend with Milkmaid and mango essence. (Mixer may be used for a smooth product.)

3. Fold in curd and chill till almost frozen.

Amrakhand

Seviyan

Seviyan

Preparation Time : 5 minutes

Cooking Time : 10 minutes

To serve 6-8

Ingredients

Milkmaid : $1/_2$ tin
Seviyan : 50 gm
Milk : $1/_2$ litre
Raisins : 2 tbsp
Nuts : 2 tbsp
Elaichi : 2, finely powdered

Method

1. Bring milk to boil. Add Milkmaid, *seviyan* and *elaichi*.

2. Cook for 2 to 3 minutes and top with raisins and nuts.

3. Serve hot.

Quick Tip

Roast seviyan lightly in 1 to 2 tsp of ghee before adding milk, if it is not the roasted variety.

14

Malai Jamun

Preparation Time : 10-15 minutes

Cooking Time : 30 minutes

To serve 8

Ingredients

For Jamuns :

Paneer : 100 gm
Maida : 7 heaped tsp
Baking powder : $^1/_2$ tsp
Oil for frying

For Syrup :

Sugar : $^1/_2$ cup
Water : $1^1/_2$ cup

For Malai :

Milkmaid : $^1/_2$ tin
Milk : 2 cups
Maida : 1 heaped tsp
Elaichi : 2, powdered
Silver leaf : 1

Method

Sugar Syrup

1. Heat sugar and water together to boil. Keep aside.

Jamuns

1. Knead *paneer* till it becomes soft and has no grain.

2. Add m*aida* and baking powder. Knead and mix well.

3. Heat oil in a kadai. Roll out *paneer* mixture into balls.

4. Deep fry *paneer* balls on slow medium heat till golden brown.

5. Cool the fried jamuns for 2 to 3 minutes. Then soak in syrup for 20 to 30 minutes.

Malai

1. Mix Milkmaid, milk and *maida* in a pan. Bring to boil stirring constantly. Cook for 2 to 3 minutes and remove from fire. Add *elaichi* powder.

To Serve

1. Remove jamuns from the syrup. Arrange in a serving bowl. Pour *malai* over the jamuns and top with silver leaf.

2. Serve chilled.

Kesari Bhaat

Preparation Time : 5 minutes

Cooking Time : 20 minutes

To serve 8

Ingredients

Milkmaid : 1 tin
Rice : 1 cup
Ghee : $^1/_2$ cup
Water : 4 cups
Orange colour : $^1/_2$ tsp
Kesar : $^1/_2$ tsp, powdered
Cashewnuts : 10-12
Edible camphor : few grains

Method

1. Wash rice and put in a strainer to drain water. Soak *kesar* in a little water.

2. Heat *ghee* in a heavy bottomed kadai and fry the wet rice till pinkish in colour.

3. Add 4 cups water, *kesar* and bring to boil. Reduce flame and cook covered, till rice is well softened.

4. Add Milkmaid and cook for another 2 to 3 minutes. Remove from fire. Add colour and camphor.

5. Garnish with fried cashewnuts and serve hot or cold as desired.

Quick Tip

Amount of water needed for cooking rice depends upon the quality of rice and may be varied slightly.

Mithai

Kesari

Pinnies

Kalakand

Coconut Burfee

Besan Halwa

Egg Halwa

Coconut Laddoo

Moong Dal Halwa

Malpua

Kesari

Preparation Time : 5 minutes

Cooking Time : 20 minutes

To serve 8

Ingredients

Milkmaid : $1/_2$ tin
Sooji : 1 cup
Ghee : $3/_4$ cup
Water : 2 cups
Kesari powder : 1 tsp
Cashewnuts : 8-10 ⎫
Raisins : $1^1/_2$ tbsp ⎬ (optional)
⎭

Method

1. Heat *ghee* in a kadai.

2. Fry cashewnuts and raisins till light brown and keep aside.

3. Add *sooji* to the remaining *ghee* and fry till light brown.

4. Add *kesari* powder dissolved in 2 cups of water. Keep stirring.

5. Reduce heat. When all the water has been absorbed, add Milkmaid. Stir well till traces of *ghee* begin to show at the sides of the pan.

6. Spread on a greased plate, top with nuts and raisins if desired.

7. Cut into diamond shaped pieces.

8. Serve warm or cold.

Quick Tip

A few drops of liquid orange-red colour may be used if kesari powder is not available.

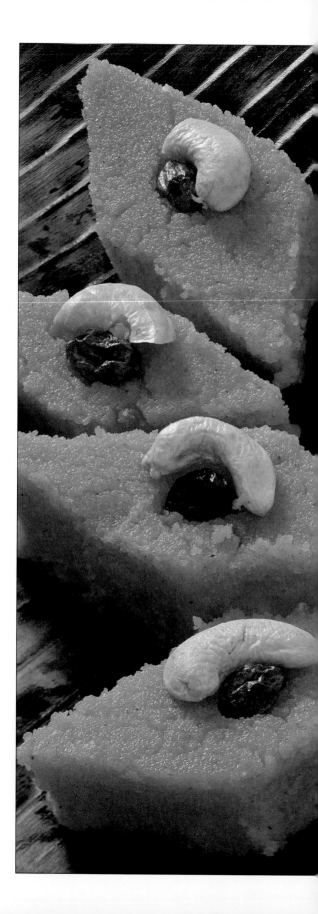

Kesari

Pinnies

Pinnies

Preparation Time : 5 minutes

Cooking Time : 20 minutes

Makes 20 Pinnies

Ingredients

Milkmaid : $\frac{1}{2}$ tin
Whole wheat flour : 400 gm
Powdered sugar : 100 gm
Ghee : 150 gm
Almonds : 50 gm (coarsely ground)
A few blanched almonds and pista for decorating

Method

1. Rub *ghee* into the flour to get bread crumb consistency.

2. Fry on medium fire till it turns medium brown. Remove from fire and cool for 5 minutes.

3. Add powdered sugar, almonds and mix thoroughly.

4. Add Milkmaid in small quantities to get a mixture which is neither too dry nor too wet.

5. Form into oval pinnies and leave to cool.

6. Serve decorated with blanched almonds.

Kalakand

Preparation Time : 5-10 minutes

Cooking Time : 10 minutes

Makes $^3/_4$ kg

Ingredients

Milkmaid : 1 tin
Paneer : $^1/_2$ kg
Elaichi : 3-4, powdered
Full cream milk powder : 2 heaped tbsp
Silver leaf : 1

Method

1. Mash *paneer* coarsely and add milk powder to it. Add Milkmaid and mix.

2. Heat the mixture in a thick bottomed pan. Cook on medium heat with constant stirring till the mixture becomes thick. (8 to 10 minutes)

3. Remove from fire and spread onto a greased plate. Sprinkle *elaichi* powder.

4. Top with silver leaf.

5. Cool and cut into squares.

Kalakand

Coconut Burfee

Preparation Time : 5 minutes

Cooking Time : 20 minutes

Makes $^3/_4$ kg

Ingredients

Milkmaid : 1 tin
Coconut : 300 gm, desiccated
Full cream milk powder : 100 gm
Milk : $^1/_2$ cup
Red colour : few drops

Method

1. Pour Milkmaid, coconut powder, milk and milk powder into a thick bottomed kadai and mix well.

2. Heat the mixture, stirring constantly, so that it does not stick to the bottom of the pan.

3. Once heated, cook on a slow fire till the mixture starts leaving the sides of the kadai (7 to 10 minutes). Remove from fire.

4. Divide the mixture into 2 portions. Spread out one portion evenly onto a greased plate.

5. To the other portion, add a few drops of red colour. Mix well to get a pale pink colour. Spread on top of the white layer and leave to cool.

6. Cut into squares, when cool.

Besan Halwa

Preparation Time : 5 minutes

Cooking Time : 15-20 minutes

To serve 5

Ingredients

Milkmaid : $^3/_4$ tin
Besan : 1 cup
Coconut : 1 cup, grated
Ghee : 1 cup
Nuts (optional)

Method

1. Heat *ghee* in a kadai. Add *besan* and fry on low heat till it becomes brown.

2. Add Milkmaid and grated coconut. Mix well. Stir constantly on a low flame till the mixture thickens and traces of *ghee* begin to show on the sides of the pan.

3. Pour into a thali and top with nuts (optional). Cut into pieces when cool.

Quick Tip

To get a grainy texture replace one tablespoon of besan with 1 tablespoon of sooji.

Egg Halwa

Preparation Time : 5 minutes

Cooking Time : 15-20 minutes

To serve 5-6

Ingredients

Milkmaid : $^3/_4$ tin
Eggs : 6, lightly beaten
Honey : $^1/_4$ cup
Milk : $^1/_2$ cup
Ghee : 1 tbsp
Almonds : 50 gm (blanched and grounded)
Raisins: 50 gm

Method

1. Combine all the ingredients and mix well.

2. Cook in a thick bottomed pan over medium heat, stirring constantly till the mixture becomes thick and leaves the sides of the pan.

3. Serve hot or cold.

Coconut Laddoo

Preparation Time : 5 minutes

Cooking Time : 10-15 minutes

Makes 20 Laddoos

Ingredients

Milkmaid : 1 tin
Desiccated coconut powder : $3^1/_2$- 4 cups

Method

1. Keep aside 50 gm coconut powder.

2. Add remaining coconut powder to Milkmaid and cook on a slow fire till the mixture leaves the sides of the pan (approx 5 minutes).

3. Cool and roll into small laddoos with buttered (oiled) hands. Roll in coconut powder and serve.

Moong Dal Halwa

Preparation Time : 1 hour

Cooking Time : 20 minutes

To serve 10-12

Ingredients

Milkmaid : 1 tin
Milk : 3 cups
Moong dal : 1 cup
(dhuli)
Ghee : 1 cup

Elaichi powder : $^1/_2$ tsp
Almonds : 3 tbsp (optional)
Raisins : 3 tbsp
Silver leaf : 1
Nutmeg : $^1/_2$ tsp

Method

1. Clean and soak *dal* for 30 minutes to 1 hour. Drain and grind to a fine paste.

2. Fry the *dal* paste in *ghee* on slow fire till the colour becomes golden brown.

3. Add milk and cook on a slow fire, stirring continuously, till milk dries up. Add Milkmaid and stir till consistency of halwa is reached.

4. Mix well and turn out onto a flat dish. Add almonds, raisins, *elaichi* powder and nutmeg.

5. Top with silver leaf.

Malpua

Preparation Time : 15 minutes

Cooking Time : 20 minutes

To serve 20

Ingredients

Malpua :
Milkmaid : $^1/_2$ tin
Sooji : 100 gm
Maida : 50 gm
Paneer : 50 gm
Water : 1 cup
Oil for frying
A pinch of baking powder

Sugar Syrup :
Sugar : $1^1/_2$ cups
Water : 2 cups

Method

Sugar Syrup

1. Put sugar and water in a pan and bring to a boil. Keep aside.

Malpua

1. Combine Milkmaid, *sooji*, *maida*, water and baking powder. Mix well and leave for 10 to 15 minutes.

2. Crumble *paneer* very finely and add to the above mixture. Beat well.

3. Heat oil in a frying pan. Pour 1 tbsp of batter to make a small, flat malpua about $2^1/_2$" to 3" in diameter.

4. Fry till both sides get evenly browned and the edges crisp.

5. Remove and soak in syrup for $^1/_2$ minute.

6. Remove from syrup and serve hot.

Quick Tip

To make approx 200 gm of paneer from milk, use 1 litre milk. Bring to boil and add lemon juice or curd or whey water to curdle.

Bengali Delights

Paatishapta

Coconut Sandesh

Ice-Cream Sandesh

Sandesh

Malai Sandesh

Tutti Frooti Sandesh

Channar Payesh

Channar Puli

Bhapa Dahi

Paatishapta

Preparation Time : 5 minutes

Cooking Time : 20 minutes

Makes 20 Paatishaptas

Ingredients

Milkmaid : $^1/_2$ tin
Maida : 1 cup
Rice : 4 tbsp soaked
Soda bicarbonate : 1 pinch
Water to make a thin batter
Ghee/oil for frying
Fresh coconut : $1^1/_2$ cups, grated
Nuts and raisins chopped (optional)

Method

1. Mix Milkmaid, coconut, nuts and raisins evenly.

2. Blend *maida*, rice flour, soda and water to make a smooth batter.

3. In a frying pan, heat 1 tsp *ghee*. Add 2 tbsp of batter and swirl the pan around to coat evenly.

4. When the batter turns creamy brown, place a little coconut and Milkmaid filling at one end and roll over to the other end. Remove and serve.

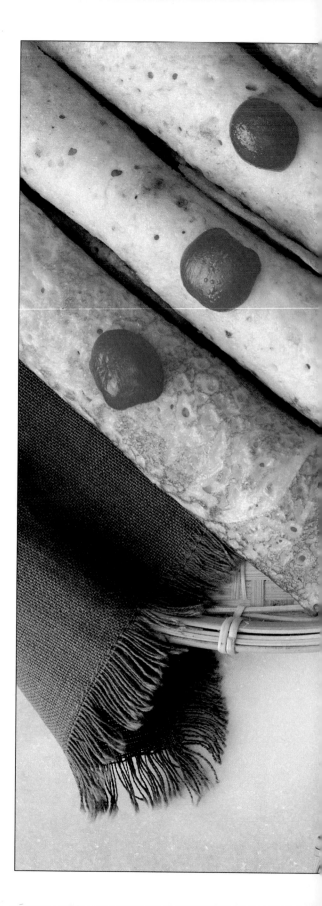

Paatishapta

Coconut Sandesh

Preparation Time : 5 minutes

Cooking Time : 30 minutes

To serve 10

Ingredients

Milkmaid : $^1/_2$ tin
Paneer : $^1/_4$ kg
Full cream milk powder : 2 heaped tbsp
Coconut powder : 100 gm
Powdered sugar : 1 tbsp

Method

1. Blend all ingredients except coconut powder into a smooth paste.

2. Heat the mixture in a thick bottomed pan.

3. Once heated thoroughly, reduce flame. Add coconut powder and cook on slow heat, stirring continuously for 15 to 20 minutes or till dry enough.

4. Pour onto a greased plate and cool.

5. When cool, cut into desired size or shape into shell using mould.

Ice-Cream Sandesh

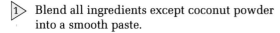

Preparation Time : 10 minutes

No cooking required

To serve 6

Ingredients

Milkmaid : $^1/_4$ tin
Paneer : $^1/_4$ kg
Full cream milk powder : 3 heaped tbsp
Malai (cream) : 2 tbsp, whipped

Method

1. Knead *paneer* well with milk powder.

2. Add Milkmaid and blend till creamy.

3. Mix in whipped cream. Spread in an ice tray to $^1/_2$" to $^3/_4$" thickness and freeze.

4. Cut into pieces and serve chilled.

Sandesh

Preparation Time : 5 minutes

Cooking Time : 30 minutes

To serve 10

Ingredients

Milkmaid : 1 tin
Paneer : $^1/_2$ kg
Full cream milk powder : 2 heaped tbsp
Powdered sugar : 2 tbsp
Maida : 1 heaped tbsp

Method

1. Blend all the ingredients to get a smooth paste. (You could use a mixer).

2. Heat the mixture in a thick bottomed pan.

3. Once heated, reduce flame and cook on slow heat, stirring continuously for 15 to 20 minutes or till dry enough.

4. Pour onto a greased plate and cool.

5. Cut into desired shapes.

Variations

For Kesar Sandesh, blend $^1/_2$ tsp of *kesar* soaked in $^1/_2$ tsp water with all the ingredient in step 1.

For Mango Sandesh, add $^1/_4$ tsp mango flavour and 2 to 3 drops of yellow colour to the mixture after step 3. Mix well and pour onto a greased plate and cool.

Quick Tips

If kesar is not available use orange-red food colour and saffron essence.

Mixer may be used to knead paneer and maida into a soft dough.

Malai Sandesh

Preparation Time : 5 minutes

Cooking Time : 40 minutes

To serve 8

Ingredients

For Sandesh :

Milkmaid : $^1/_2$ tin
Paneer : $^1/_4$ kg
Full cream milk powder : 1 heaped tbsp
Powdered sugar : 1 tbsp
Maida : $^1/_2$ heaped tbsp

For Malai :

Milkmaid : $^1/_2$ tin
Milk : 2 cups
Cornflour : 1 tsp
Elaichi : 2, powdered
Silver leaf : 1

Method

For Sandesh :

1. Blend all the ingredients together to get a smooth paste. (You can use a mixer).

2. Heat the mixture in a thick bottomed pan/ kadai.

3. Once heated, reduce flame and cook on slow fire stirring continuously. Cook for 15 to 20 minutes or till dry enough.

4. Pour onto a greased plate. Cool, cut into desired shapes and sizes or shape into oval rounds with hand.

For Malai :

1. Mix together Milkmaid and milk. Bring to boil.

2. Add *elaichi* powder and cornflour made into a paste with little milk. Stir continuously. Cook for 3 to 5 minutes on slow heat.

3. Arrange Sandesh pieces in a serving dish and pour *malai* on top. Decorate with silver leaf and serve chilled.

Quick Tip

Cooking the paneer at high temperature makes it tough and leathery and ruins the texture and feel of the product.

Sandesh

Tutti Frooti Sandesh

Preparation Time : 5 minutes

Cooking Time : 30 minutes

To serve 10

Ingredients

Milkmaid : $^1/_2$ tin
Paneer : $^1/_4$ kg
Full cream milk powder : 2 heaped tbsp
Powdered sugar : 1 tbsp
Maida : 1 tbsp
Crystallised peel and fruit of different
colours (chopped fine) : 50 gm

Method

1. Blend all the ingredients except the crystallised peel into a smooth paste.

2. Transfer to a thick bottomed pan and keep on fire, stirring continuously.

3. Once the mixture is heated thoroughly, reduce flame. Cook on slow fire, stirring continuously, for 15 to 20 minutes or till the mixture is dry enough.

4. Add the crystallised fruit and cook for another 2 minutes.

5. Remove from fire and pour onto a greased plate. Leave to cool.

6. When cool, cut into desired shapes.

Quick Tips

Mixer may be used to get a smooth paste.

To knead paneer to a smooth paste rub in a thali with palms of the hand or rub through a sieve or blend in a mixer or a food processor.

Channar Payesh

Preparation Time : 5 minutes

Cooking Time : 15 minutes

To serve 6

Ingredients

Milkmaid : 1 tin
Paneer (crumbled) : 250 gm
Milk : $^1/_2$ litre
Cornflour : 1 tbsp
Nuts and raisins : 1 tbsp
Rose water : 2-3 drops
Rose petals : few } (optional)

Method

1. In a kadai boil milk. Add Milkmaid and cool till just warm.

2. Add this mixture to the grated *paneer*, stir well, a little at a time until all the milk is used up.

3. Pour into a suitable sized serving bowl. Decorate with nuts, raisins and rose petals. Sprinkle rose water.

4. Chill and serve.

Channar Payesh

Channar Puli

Preparation Time : 5-10 minutes

Cooking Time : 25 minutes

Makes 30 Channar Pulis

Ingredients

Milkmaid : $^1/_2$ tin
Paneer : 250 gm
Maida : 6-7 tbsp
Baking powder : $^1/_2$ tsp
Ghee : 1 tbsp
Vanaspati ghee for frying

Syrup :
Sugar : $1^1/_2$ cups
Water : 2 cups

Method

1. Knead Milkmaid, *paneer*, *maida* and baking powder with *ghee* to a smooth sticky dough.

2. Make sugar syrup with sugar and water.

3. Heat *ghee* in a kadai. Roll out *paneer* mixture into elongated shapes and deep fry on medium heat till golden brown.

4. Soak in syrup and serve hot.

Bhapa Dahi

Preparation Time : 25-30 minutes

Cooking Time : 20-25 minutes

To serve 8-10

Ingredients

Milkmaid : 1 tin
Nuts and raisins : 25 gm (optional)
Curd : 3 cups
A pinch of elaichi powder

Method

1. Tie curd in a muslin cloth. Hang for 25 to 30 minutes to remove excess water.

2. Add Milkmaid and *elaichi* powder. Cover the bowl with foil or grease proof paper.

3. Place the bowl in another pan of boiling water and steam for 15 to 20 minutes. Cool.

4. Decorate with nuts and raisins. Serve chilled.

Quick Tip

Pressure cooker without weight may be used for steaming.

Channar Puli and Bhapa Dahi

Festive Times

Shahi Tukre

❧

Pista Burfee

❧

Kaju Burfee

❧

Rabri

❧

Channa Dal Payasam

❧

Badam Kheer

❧

Malai Peda

❧

Thandai

❧

Malai Laddoo

Shahi Tukre

Preparation Time : 10 minutes

Cooking Time : 15 minutes

To serve 10-12

Ingredients

Milkmaid : $^1/_2$ tin
Bread : 8 slices
Milk : 1 cup
Cornflour : 1 tbsp
Elaichi powder : 1 tsp
Nuts : 1 tbsp, chopped
Oil/ghee to fry

Syrup :
Sugar : 1 cup
Water : 1 cup

Method

1. Make a paste of cornflour with some milk. Mix Milkmaid with the rest of the milk.

2. Bring milk mixture to boil. Add cornflour paste. Cook stirring constantly until thick. Add *elaichi* powder.

3. Prepare syrup by boiling water and sugar together. Strain and keep aside.

4. Cut bread slices into two and deep fry in *ghee* till golden brown.

5. Immediately put the fried bread into sugar syrup. Dip for a minute. Remove from syrup, and arrange in a serving dish.

6. Top each piece of bread with 1 tbsp mixture of Milkmaid and nuts. Chill.

7. Serve chilled.

Quick Tip

Soak in sugar syrup for a little longer if softer tukres are preferred.

Shahi Tukre

Pista and Kaju Burfee

Pista Burfee

Preparation Time : 10 minutes

Cooking Time : 10 minutes

Makes ¹/₂ kg

Ingredients

Milkmaid : ³/₄ tin
Paneer : 150 gm
Khoa : 150 gm
Maida : 50 gm
Pista : 75 gm, finely powdered

Method

1. Mash *paneer* and *khoa* till smooth. Blend in Milkmaid and *maida* (mixer may be used). Add powdered *pista*.

2. Transfer to a thick bottomed vessel. Cook on slow fire till the mixture becomes thick and forms a ball.

3. Pour onto a lightly greased tray and spread evenly to about ¹/₂" thickness. Cool for 4 to 5 hours and cut into 2" square pieces.

Kaju Burfee

Preparation Time : 5 minutes

Cooking Time : 30 minutes

Makes $^1/_2$ kg

Ingredients

Milkmaid : $^1/_2$ tin   Maida : 50 gm
Kaju : 150 gm   Milk : $^1/_2$ cup
Khoa : 150 gm

Method

1▷ Crush *kaju* to a fine powder.

2▷ Put all the ingredients together and grind to a smooth paste.

3▷ Transfer to a thick bottomed kadai and cook on a slow fire till the mixture starts leaving the sides and forms a ball.

4▷ Put the mixture in a tray and roll out thinly ($^1/_8$"). Cool and cut into diamond shapes.

Rabri

Preparation Time : 5 minutes

Cooking Time : 10 minutes

To serve 8

Ingredients

Milkmaid : 1 tin
Milk : 4 cups
Paneer : 200 gm
Maida : 1 tbsp
Elaichi : 3, powdered
Chopped nuts : 2 tbsp

Method

1▷ Crumble *paneer* coarsely.

2▷ Make a paste of *maida* with 3 to 4 tbsp milk. Combine Milkmaid and the rest of milk and bring to boil.

3▷ Add *maida* paste to milk stirring continuously. Reduce flame and cook for 5 minutes.

4▷ Add chopped nuts, *paneer* and *elaichi* powder. Remove from fire.

5▷ Cool and refrigerate. Serve chilled.

Channa Dal Payasam

Preparation Time : 1 hour

Cooking Time : 30-40 minutes

To serve 10-12

Ingredients

Milkmaid : 1 tin
Channa dal : 1 cup
Jaggery : 100 gm
Elaichi powder : $^1/_4$ tsp
Fresh coconut : 1
Cashewnuts : 10
Ghee : 1 tbsp

Method

1▷ Cook *dal* in enough of water till soft and well done. Mash with the back of a large ladle.

2▷ Heat jaggery with 1 cup of water to dissolve. Strain and keep aside.

3▷ Grate coconut. Reserve 2 tbsp of scrapings for decoration.

4▷ Pour 1 cup of boiling water over the remaining coconut and leave for 30 minutes. Strain to get 1 cup of thick milk.

5▷ To the coconut scrapings add another 2 cups of hot water and keep aside for 15 minutes.

6▷ Strain through a muslin cloth to get another 2 cups of thin milk.

7▷ Mix the jaggery syrup, mashed *dal* and 2 cups of thin milk and heat with constant stirring. Cook for 3 to 5 minutes. Add Milkmaid and stir well.

8▷ Remove from fire and add 1 cup of thick coconut milk.

9▷ Fry cashewnuts in *ghee*. Add to the payasam along with the *ghee*.

10▷ Top with coconut scrapings and *elaichi* powder and serve.

Quick Tip

Dal may be cooked in a pressure cooker. Adjust quantity of water if a pressure cooker is used.

Badam Kheer and Channa Dal Payasam

Badam Kheer

Preparation Time : 45 minutes

Cooking Time : 20 minutes

To serve 10-12

Ingredients

Milkmaid : 1 tin
Milk : 1 litre
Cashewnuts : 50 gm
Almonds : 50 gm
Almond essence : $^1/_4$ tsp

Method

1. Blanch almonds and remove skin.

2. Soak almonds and cashewnuts in 2 cups of hot milk for 30 minutes. Grind to a paste along with milk.

3. Heat the remaining milk to boil. Add Milkmaid and the ground almond paste and cook for another 5 minutes with constant stirring.

4. Remove from fire and add almond essence.

5. Serve hot or cold.

44

Malai Peda

Preparation Time : 5 minutes

Cooking Time : 10-15 minutes

Makes 20 Pedas

Ingredients

Milkmaid : 1 tin
Milk : 1$^1/_2$ cups
Cornflour : 1 tsp
Citric acid : $^1/_4$ tsp
Elaichi : 4-5, powdered
Ghee : 1 tbsp
Yellow colour : A few drops

Method

1. Heat *ghee* in a pan. Add Milkmaid, milk and citric acid dissolved in a little water. Continue heating and allow to curdle.

2. Make a paste of cornflour with 2 tbsp water. Add to the milk mixture after it curdles.

3. Continue cooking on slow/medium heat till the mixture leaves the sides of the pan.

4. Add colour and mix well.

5. Empty the contents onto a dish and shape into pedas. Decorate with *elaichi* powder.

Malai Peda

Thandai

Thandai

Preparation Time : 10 minutes

No cooking required

To serve 12

Ingredients

Milkmaid : $^1/_2$ tin
Milk : $1^1/_2$ litre
Almonds : 8-10, soaked and peeled
Peppercorns : 5-6
Elaichi : 3-4
Saunf : 2 tsp
Khus essence : 1 tsp
Crushed ice

Method

1. Grind soaked and peeled almonds, *elaichi* and *saunf* to a fine paste. Blend with other ingredients till well mixed. Strain.

2. Half fill each glass with crushed ice and top up with the above mixture.

3. Serve garnished with rose petals.

Quick Tip

2 tbsp of poppy seeds or Khus-Khus can be used in place of Khus essence.

Malai Laddoo

Preparation Time : 20 minutes

Cooking Time : 10 minutes

Makes 10 Laddoos

Ingredients

Milkmaid : $^1/_2$ cup
Paneer : 250 gm
Kewra essence : 2-3 drops
Yellow food colour : 4-5 drops
Elaichi : 2
Silver leaf : 1

Method

1. Mash *paneer* well.

2. Add Milkmaid and cook on slow fire stirring constantly.

3. Cook till the mixture thickens and starts leaving the sides of the kadai.

4. Add colour and essence. Remove from fire. Mix well and pour this *malai* on a plate.

5. Allow the *malai* to cool.

6. Make laddoos of the *malai*, sprinkle *elaichi* powder and serve decorated with silver leaf on top.

Malai Laddoo

47

Anytime Treats

Vanilla Fudge

Chocolate Fudge

Lemon Tarts

Scones

Drop Scones

Caramel Squares

Brownies

Cream Puffs

Chocolate Walnut Spread

Butterscotch Spread

Doughnuts

Black Forest Cake

Banana Ring Cake

Cold Coffee

Butter Cookies

Gingerbread

Vanilla Fudge

Preparation Time : 5 minutes

Cooking Time : 20 minutes

Makes 16 squares

Ingredients

Milkmaid : 1 tin
Sugar : 1 cup
Butter : 125 gm
Maida : $^3/_4$ cup
Vanilla essence : 1 tsp

Method

1> Put all the ingredients together except vanilla essence in a thick bottomed kadai. Mix well and heat.

2> Once the mixture is heated and sugar melted, cook on a slow fire till thick. (Soft ball stage).

3> Remove from fire.

4> Add vanilla essence and mix well. Pour onto a greased plate. Smoothen the top and cool.

5> When cool cut into squares.

Chocolate Fudge

Preparation Time : 5 minutes

Cooking Time : 20-25 minutes

Makes 16 squares

Ingredients

Milkmaid : 1 tin
Powdered sugar : $^1/_2$ cup
Cocoa : $^3/_4$ cup
Walnuts (broken) : 1 cup

Butter : 125 gm
Maida : 2 tbsp

Method

1> Mix all the ingredients except walnuts in a kadai and heat.

2> Once heated, cook on slow fire for 10 to 15 minutes till the mixture thickens and starts moving in a mass (soft ball stage). Stir in walnuts, broken coarsely.

3> Pour onto a greased plate and smoothen surface. Cool.

4> When cool cut into 2" squares.

Lemon Tarts

Preparation Time : 10 minutes

Cooking Time : 15 minutes

To serve 7

Ingredients

Pastry :

Maida : 200 gm
Salted butter : 100 gm (or salt free butter
                  + $^1/_4$ tsp. salt).
Cold water : 5-6 tbsp

Filling :

Milkmaid : $^1/_4$ tin
Lemon : 1, large
Rind of $^1/_2$ lemon
Lemon yellow colour : few drops
Cherries for decoration

Method

For Pastry

1> Cut cold butter into small pieces. Using a palette knife rub butter into the *maida*.

2> Sprinkle cold water over *maida* and using a palette knife combine into a ball.

3> With minimum handling, roll into $^1/_8$" thick pastry. Using a cutter, cut out rounds $^1/_2$" more in diameter than the tart case.

4> Line the lightly greased tart cases with pastry and bake blind at 180° C for 10 to 15 minutes.

5> Allow to cool.

For Filling

1> Beat Milkmaid, lemon juice, and rind together. Add a little colour and mix in well.

For Serving

1> Fill the tarts with the filling.

2> Serve topped with cherries and lemon rind.

Quick Tip

Rubbing in of solid fat in maida is made easier and uniform if two palette knives are used.

Scones

Preparation Time : 10 minutes

Cooking Time : 30 minutes

To serve 15

Ingredients

Milkmaid : $^1/_2$ tin   Baking powder : $1^1/_2$ tsp
Milk : 1 cup   Butter : 125 gm
Maida : 500 gm   Egg : 1
Strawberry/Raspberry jam : for filling

Method

1. Sift together *maida* and baking powder into a bowl.

2. Rub in butter till mixture resembles bread crumbs.

3. Break the egg and drop into the *maida*.

4. Mix Milkmaid and milk together. Add it to the *maida* mixture to make a soft dough.

5. Roll out to $^1/_2$" thickness. Cut into rounds of $2^1/_2$" to 3" diameter and bake in a preheated oven at 150° C for 30 minutes.

6. Split when still hot and spread jam. Serve warm.

Quick Tip

When rubbing fat into maida, use only fingertips.

Drop Scones

Preparation Time : 5 minutes

Cooking Time : 10 minutes

To serve 6

Ingredients

Milkmaid : $^1/_2$ tin   Salt-free butter for frying
Maida : 1 cup   Honey : 6 tbsp
Eggs : 2   Baking powder : $^1/_4$ tsp

Method

1. Put Milkmaid, *maida*, eggs and baking powder into a bowl and beat well to get a thick batter.

2. Heat butter and drop ladlefuls of the batter to get flat, round scones of $2^1/_2$" diameter.

3. Fry lightly on both sides on slow heat. Remove from pan and top with 1 tsp of honey. Serve warm.

Caramel Squares

Preparation Time : 15 minutes

Cooking Time : 40 minutes

Makes 20 squares

Ingredients

Base :

Maida : 225 gm
Butter : 150 gm
Powdered sugar : 100 gm

Filling :

Milkmaid : $^1/_2$ tin
Butter : 50 gm

Topping :

Chopped cashewnut : $^1/_2$ cup
Chopped chocolate bar : 50 gm

Method

For Base

1. Lightly grease a baking tray. Preheat oven to 120° C.

2. Cream butter and sugar together.

3. Add sifted *maida* and mix in.

4. Press $^2/_3$ of the mixture into $^1/_8$" thick layer in a greased 20 cm x 30 cm tin. Put the remaining mixture into the refrigerator.

For Filling

1. In a saucepan, carefully melt butter. Remove from fire.

2. Add Milkmaid and mix well.

3. Spread the filling evenly over the base.

For Topping

1. Mix together the chopped chocolate and cashewnuts. Sprinkle over the filling.

2. Sprinkle *maida* mixture from the refrigerator over nuts and chocolate.

3. Bake at 120° C for 20 to 30 minutes.

4. Cool and cut into squares.

5. Can be served immediately or can be stored for 2 to 3 days.

Quick Tip

While heating chocolate mixture always heat on low to medium heat otherwise the chocolate burns.

Brownies

Brownies

Preparation Time : 15-20 minutes

Cooking Time : 30 minutes

To serve 8-10

Ingredients

Milkmaid : $^1/_4$ tin
Maida : 120 gm
Butter : 120 gm
Cocoa : 90 gm
Sugar : 50 gm
Eggs : 2
Milk : $^1/_3$ cup
Baking powder : $^1/_2$ tsp.

Icing :

Milkmaid : $^1/_4$ tin
Cocoa sieved : 30 gm
Butter : 50 gm

Method

1. Grease and dust the baking tray with *maida*.

2. Preset oven at 160° C.

3. Sieve together *maida*, cocoa and baking powder.

4. Beat butter and sugar until light and creamy. Add eggs a little at a time, beating well after each addition.

5. Fold sieved ingredients into the above mixture alternating with Milkmaid and milk. Mix well and pour into a greased tray.

6. Bake at 160° C for 25 to 30 minutes until centre of the sponge springs back when lightly pressed. Allow to cool in tray.

For Icing

1. Melt butter for icing. Add cocoa. Cook over low heat for 1 minute. Remove from heat and add Milkmaid. Mix thoroughly. Spread over cake in tray and leave to set. Cut into squares and serve.

53

Cream Puffs

Preparation Time : 10 minutes

Cooking Time : 40 minutes

To serve 7

Ingredients

Butter : 80 gm
Water : $1^1/_4$ cup
Sifted maida : 180 gm
Eggs : 4
Vanilla essence : 1 tsp

Filling :

Milkmaid : $^1/_2$ tin
Cornflour : 2 tbsp
Milk : $1^1/_4$ cup
Egg yolk : 1
Butter : $^1/_2$ tsp
Vanilla essence : $^1/_4$ tsp

Method

1. Lightly grease a baking tray. Heat oven to 200° C.

2. Place water and butter in a saucepan. Heat till butter melts and water is boiling. Reduce heat and add *maida* all at once. Beat well until mixture leaves the sides of saucepan and forms into a ball. Remove from fire. Cool for 2 to 3 minutes.

3. Beat eggs lightly and add gradually to cooled paste. Add essence and beat well.

4. Place small spoonfuls of pastry onto baking tray. Bake for 30 to 35 minutes at 200° C or until golden brown. Cool.

For Filling

1. Mix together Milkmaid and milk. Make a paste of cornflour in little milk.

2. Heat milk to boil. Add cornflour paste and cook over low heat, stirring constantly until custard is fairly thick. Stir in egg yolk, butter and essence. Cool, stirring occasionally to prevent a skin forming.

3. Slit the cream puffs and fill with the cooled custard. Serve.

Cream Puffs

Chocolate Walnut Spread

Preparation Time : 5 minutes

Cooking Time : 5 minutes

Makes 1 jam bottle

Ingredients

Milkmaid : 1 tin
Cocoa : 4 tbsp
Chocolate bar broken into pieces : 50 gm
Chopped walnuts : 2 tbsp
Butter : 1 tbsp

Method

1. Melt butter, cocoa and chocolate together over gentle heat.

2. Mix in Milkmaid gradually, stirring well.

3. Cook over low heat till thick. Add walnuts. Cool and store in bottle.

Butterscotch Spread

Preparation Time : 5 minutes

Cooking Time : 15-20 minutes

Makes 1 jam bottle

Ingredients

Milkmaid : 1 tin
Butter : 2 tbsp
Sugar : 1 tbsp

Method

1. Heat sugar till it melts and caramelises to a golden brown colour. Immediately add butter and mix well.

2. Gradually add Milkmaid, stirring well to avoid lumps. Cook for 10 to 15 minutes on low heat or till thick.

3. Cool and store in bottle.

Doughnuts

Preparation Time : 60 minutes

Cooking Time : 10 minutes

Makes 12 Doughnuts

Ingredients

Milkmaid : 2 tbsp
Milk : $1/2$ cup
Maida : 250 gm
Egg : 1
Butter : 1 tbsp
Dried yeast : 2 tsp
Salt : a pinch
Jam : 2 tbsp

For coating :
Powdered sugar : 50 gm
Cinnamon powder : $1/2$ tsp

Method

1. Mix 2 to 3 tbsp Milkmaid and milk together. Warm over a pan of hot water. Blend in yeast and 2 tbsp of *maida*. Leave at room temperature for 20 to 30 minutes to ferment.

2. Mix salt and remaining *maida* together. Add to fermented yeast mixture along with beaten egg and melted butter. Mix well.

3. Knead dough well on a lightly floured table and divide into 12 equal rounds. Cover each with a greased polythene sheet and leave to rise for about 30 minutes at room temperature.

4. Remove polythene. Make a hole in the middle of each round. Fill in $1/2$ tsp of jam, pinch into shape again.

5. Deep fry in medium hot fat. Drain on absorbent paper.

6. Roll in sugar, cinnamon mixture and serve.

Quick Tips

The mixture containing yeast should be only lukewarm (38-40° C). Overheating destroys the yeast cells.

When yeast dough is left for rising, cover well with greased polythene sheet to prevent a skin forming on the surface.

If fresh yeast is used instead of dry yeast, double the quantity of yeast.

Doughnuts

Black Forest Cake

Black Forest Cake

Preparation Time : 10-15 minutes

Cooking Time : 40 minutes

To serve 12

Ingredients

Milkmaid : 1 tin
Maida : 225 gm
Butter : 125 gm
Cocoa : 3-4 heaped tbsp
Aerated cola drink : 1 bottle (200 ml)
Baking powder : 1 tsp
Soda bicarbonate : 1 tsp
Cream : 1 cup
Tinned cherries : 1 small tin
Chocolate bar : 25-40 gm

Method

1. Lightly grease and flour a baking tin. Preheat the oven to 150° C.

2. Melt the butter in a pan. Cool and add Milkmaid.

3. Sift together the *maida*, baking powder, soda and cocoa.

4. Mix the *maida* with the Milkmaid-butter mixture alternating with cola till the *maida* and cola are over.

5. Immediately pour into the prepared tin and bake for 30 to 40 minutes at 150° C.

6. Cool and slit horizontally into two.

7. Whip cream till light and fluffy. Sandwich the two layers of cake with whipped cream and destoned cherries.

8. Top with whipped cream and cherries.

9. Sprinkle generously with grated chocolate.

10. Chill and serve.

Banana Ring Cake

Preparation Time : 15 minutes

Cooking Time : 30 minutes

To serve 12

Ingredients

Milkmaid : $1/4$ tin
Maida : 200 gm
Eggs : 5, separated
Powdered sugar : 1 cup
Butter : 225 gm
Bananas : 1 cup, finely chopped
Baking powder : 1 tsp
Soda bicarbonate : 1 tsp
Salt : a pinch
Banana essence : $1/2$ tsp

Method

1. Heat oven to 180° C. Lightly grease and flour in a 25 cm ring mould.

2. Sift together *maida*, baking powder, soda and salt.

3. Cream butter and powdered sugar together until light and creamy.

4. Add yolks of eggs, one at a time, beating well after each addition.

5. Blend in Milkmaid, bananas and essence. Fold in sifted *maida*.

6. Whisk egg whites until stiff but not dry. Fold into the above mixture.

7. Turn into the prepared mould and bake for 25 to 30 minutes or until a toothpick inserted in centre of cake comes out clean.

8. Cool for 5 minutes, then remove the cake from the baking tin and cool on a wire rack.

Cold Coffee

Preparation Time : 5 minutes

No cooking required

To serve 4

Ingredients

Milkmaid : $^1/_2$ tin
Milk : 3 cups
Instant coffee : 4 tsp
Ice cubes : 8-10

Method

 Blend all the ingredients in an electric blender or use a shaker.

2. Serve immediately while still frothy.

3. Sprinkle grated chocolate or chocolate powder on top, if desired.

Cold Coffee

Butter Cookies

Butter Cookies

Preparation Time : 5 minutes

Cooking Time : 20 minutes

To serve 10

Ingredients

Milkmaid : $^1/_2$ tin
Maida : 250 gm
Butter : 150 gm
Baking powder : $1^1/_2$ tsp

Method

1. Preheat oven to 160° C.

2. Beat together Milkmaid and butter.

3. Sift together *maida* and baking powder. Add to Milkmaid mixture and make a soft dough.

4. Roll the dough to $^1/_8$" thickness. Cut into desired shapes and sizes. Place on a greased baking tray. Prick with a fork. Bake at 160° C for 15 to 20 minutes in a preheated oven.

5. Cool and store in an airtight jar.

61

Ginger Bread

Preparation Time : 15 minutes

Cooking Time : 45-50 minutes

To serve 10-12

Ingredients

Milkmaid : 1 tin
Maida : 250 gm
Fresh ginger paste : 2 tsp
Butter : 80 gm
Eggs : 2
Soda bicarbonate : $1^1/_2$ tsp
Caramel syrup : $^1/_2$ cup
(3 tbsp sugar to prepare caramel syrup).

Method

1. Grease a loaf tin and dust with *maida*. Heat oven to 160° C.

2. Preparation of caramel syrup : Heat 3 tbsp of sugar in a pan till it melts. Continue heating till all the syrup turns brown. Add $^1/_2$ cup hot water and bring to a boil. Remove from fire. Strain and cool.

3. Sift *maida* and soda together.

4. Mix together Milkmaid, butter, caramel syrup, ginger and the lightly beaten eggs.

5. Add sifted *maida* mixture and beat lightly to mix well.

6. Pour into the greased cake tin and bake for 45 to 50 minutes in a preheated oven.

7. Remove the bread from the tin. Allow to cool on a wire rack for 5 to 10 minutes.

8. Slice and serve hot with butter.

Ginger Bread

Fruity Fare

Pineapple Upside-Down Cake

Mixed Fruit Whip

Banana Milk Shake

Trifle Pudding

Fruit Flan

Fruit Mould

Orange Pudding

Mango Cheese Cake

Leechi Pancake

Apple Crumble

Apple Custard

Pineapple Upside-Down Cake

Preparation Time : 15 minutes.

Cooking Time : 30 minutes.

To serve 10

Ingredients

Milkmaid : 1 tin
Maida : 250 gm
Butter : 125 gm
Pineapple slices : 6
Baking powder : 1 tsp
Soda bicarbonate : 1 tsp
Aerated soda : 1 bottle (200 ml)
Pineapple essence : $^1/_2$ tsp
Yellow colour : $^1/_2$ tsp
Sugar for caramelisation : 5-6 tbsp

Method

1. Preheat oven to 150° C.

2. Grease an 8" square cake tin with butter. Arrange the 6 pineapple slices at the base.

3. Heat sugar in a pan till it melts and becomes brown. Pour hot caramel onto the pineapple slices and leave aside.

4. Melt butter over hot water. Cool. Add Milkmaid and beat well. Add colour and essence.

5. Sieve together *maida*, baking powder and soda bicarbonate.

6. Add 2 tbsp of *maida* to the Milkmaid mixture. Stir. Add 2 tbsp of aerated soda and beat well. Repeat, alternatively *maida* and aerated soda till all the *maida* and soda are used up.

7. Pour batter into the prepared cake tin and bake at 150° C for 30 to 40 minutes in a preheated oven.

8. Remove from oven, loosen sides of cake using a knife and immediately turn onto a plate.

Quick Tips

Do not allow pineapple upside-down cake to cool before removing from the tin. The caramelised sugar hardens and results in the cake sticking to the tin.

The cake batter should be used for baking immediately after mixing the ingredients. If the batter is allowed to stand, it loses its lightness.

Pineapple Upside-Down Cake

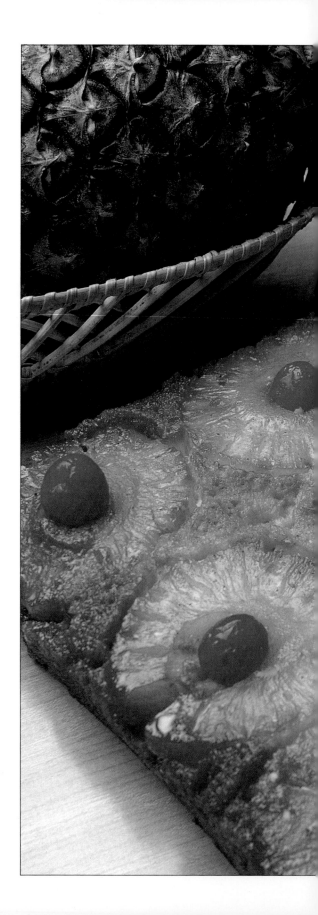

Mixed Fruit Whip

Preparation Time : 15-20 minutes

No cooking time required

To serve 8

Ingredients

Milkmaid : 1 tin
Chopped apple : 2
Chopped banana : 2
Chopped guava : 1 (seeds removed)
Skinned orange : 1
Cream : $^1/_2$ cup
Juice of 1 lemon

Method

1. Whip cream lightly and chill.

2. Mix together all the chopped fruit and the lemon juice.

3. Keep aside 2 tbsp of the chopped fruit and blend the remaining fruit in a mixer with Milkmaid till smooth. Add cream.

4. Mix in chopped fruit and serve chilled.

Quick Tip

For variety, you can make single fruits whip using any favourite fruit in season.

Banana Milk Shake

Preparation Time : 5 minutes

No cooking required

To serve 4

Ingredients

Milkmaid : $^1/_2$ tin
Milk : 3 cups
Bananas : 2
Ice cubes : 8-10

Method

1. Blend all the ingredients in an electric blender.

2. Serve immediately.

Trifle Pudding

Preparation Time : 35-40 minutes

No cooking required

To serve 8-10

Ingredients

Milkmaid : $^1/_2$ tin
Milk : 1 cup
Strawberry jelly : 1 packet
Sponge cake : $^1/_2$ kg
Cream : 1 cup
Chopped mixed seasonal fruit : 3 cups

Method

1. Prepare jelly as per instructions on the pack and leave to set.

2. Cut sponge cake into small pieces and place at the bottom of a glass serving dish.

3. Mix together Milkmaid and milk. Pour over the sponge cake.

4. Spread chopped fruit on the cake.

5. Chop set jelly and pour on top of the fruit.

6. Top with whipped cream and serve chilled.

Quick Tips

Instead of sponge cake, ordinary cake rusks may be used.

Fresh fruit, whenever mentioned may be substituted with canned sliced fruit if available.

Sprinkle all cut fruit with lemon juice to prevent browning.

Fruit Flan

Preparation Time : 30 minutes

Cooking Time : 30 minutes

To serve 10

Ingredients

Flan :

Milkmaid : 1 tin
Maida : 250 gm
Butter : 125 gm
Baking powder : 1 tsp
Soda bicarbonate : 1 tsp
Aerated soda water : 1 bottle (200 ml)
Yellow colour : $^1/_2$ tsp
Vanilla essence : $^1/_2$ tsp

Filling :

Milkmaid : $^1/_2$ tin
Lemon (large) : 2 (rind of 1 and juice of 2)
Gelatine : 1 tbsp
Water : 3-4 tbsp
Cream : 1 cup
Mixed chopped fruit : 1-2 cups

Decoration :

Cream : $^1/_4$ cup
Cherries : 2-3/any fruit pieces

Method

Flan :

1. Grease an 8" diameter flan tin with butter and set the oven at 150° C.

2. Melt butter over hot water. Cool. Add Milkmaid and beat well. Add colour and essence.

3. Sieve together *maida*, baking powder and soda bicarbonate.

4. Add 2 tbsp of *maida* to the Milkmaid mixture. Stir. Add 2 tbsp of aerated soda and beat well. Repeat, alternating *maida* and aerated soda till all the *maida* and soda are used up.

5. Pour the batter into the prepared flan tin and bake at 150° C for 30 to 40 minutes in a preheated oven.

6. Remove from oven, cool for a while. Loosen sides of cake using a knife, turn over a plate and cool completely.

Filling :

1. Soak gelatine in 3 to 4 tbsp water and dissolve over a pan of hot water.

2. Beat Milkmaid, lemon juice and rind together. Add dissolved gelatine.

3. Beat cream till light and fluffy. Fold into the Milkmaid mixture.

4. Pour half the filling into the flan case and let it set in the refrigerator.

5. Cover with chopped mixed fruit. Pour another layer of filling and set.

6. Decorate with stiffly beaten cream and cherries. Serve cold.

Fruit Mould

Preparation Time : 10 minutes

Cooking Time : 5 minutes

To serve 6

Ingredients

Milkmaid : 1 tin
Orange jelly crystals : 100 gm
Mixed seasonal fruit : 2 cups
Juice of 1 lemon.

Method

1. Dissolve jelly crystals in 300 ml boiling water. Cool to room temperature and then whisk in the Milkmaid.

2. Stir in the chopped mixed fruit and lemon juice.

3. Pour into a wet mould and leave to set.

4. When set, unmould and serve.

Quick Tips

Chill cream well before beating or beat over ice to get a smoother, light and fluffy product and to prevent sudden butter formation.

For unmoulding a jellied dessert, dip the bowl in hot water for a few seconds. Or rub the outside of the bowl/mould with a hot wet towel.

Orange Pudding

Preparation Time : 20-25 minutes

Cooking Time : 60 minutes

To serve 8

Ingredients

Milkmaid : 1 tin
Eggs : 6, separated
Oranges : 6

Method

1. Preheat oven to 160° C.

2. Make oranges into small seedless, skinless segments and mix with well beaten egg yolks and Milkmaid. Pour the mixture into an ovenproof dish.

3. Bake at 160° C for 15 minutes. Allow to cool.

4. Beat egg whites till stiff. Pile into cooled custard base and bake at 75 to 100° C for 30 to 45 minutes or till golden brown.

5. Serve hot or chilled.

Quick Tip

To get stiffly beaten egg whites make sure that the beater and the bowl are absolutely clean and non-greasy. Rub the bowl well with a teaspoon of salt and half a lemon and rinse with cold water for best results.

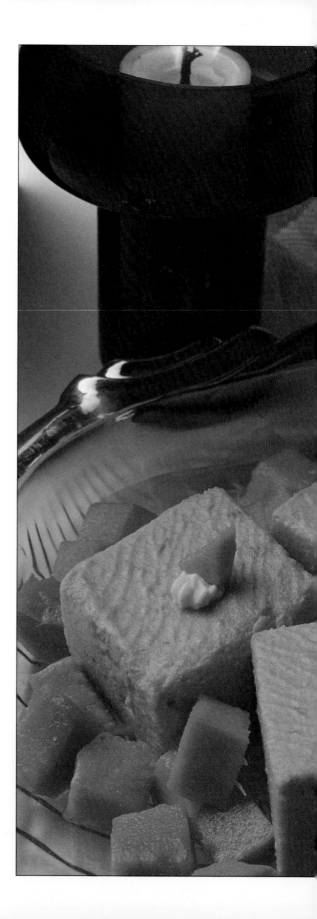

Mango Cheese Cake

Preparation Time : 15 minutes

No cooking required

To serve 8

Ingredients

Milkmaid : 1 tin
Paneer : 200 gm
Gelatine : 2 tbsp
Chopped mango : 250 gm
Mango flavour : $^1/_4$ tsp
Cream : $^1/_2$ cup

Method

1. Soak gelatine in $^1/_4$ cup water for 10 minutes. Dissolve over a pan of hot water.

2. Peel and chop mango into small pieces.

3. Mash *paneer* to a smooth paste. Blend in Milkmaid, gelatine and mango flavour. A blender may be used. Add slightly crushed mango pieces (save some for decorating) and blend again.

4. Fold in whipped cream.

5. Pour into a wet mould. Decorate with mango slices/pieces. Leave to set in the refrigerator.

6. When set, cut into squares and serve.

Quick Tip

Wetting a mould for jellied desserts makes unmoulding easier and neater.

Mango Cheese Cake

Leechi Pancake

Preparation Time : 30 minutes

Cooking Time : 30 minutes

To serve 15

Ingredients

Milkmaid : $^3/_4$ tin
Leechi : 1 kg
Maida : 100 gm
Milk : 1 cup
Salt : $^1/_4$ tsp
Cream : $^3/_4$ kg
Egg : 1
Butter for frying

Method

1. Sift *maida* and salt. Add egg and mix well.

2. Mix milk with 1 cup water. Add $^3/_4$ cup of milk and water mixture to *maida*. Beat well and keep aside for 10 to 15 minutes.

3. Chop the flesh of *leechi* into small pieces. Stew in its own juice. Cool and mix *leechis* with Milkmaid.

4. Dilute the pancake batter with the rest of the milk and water mixture.

5. Heat a heavy bottomed frying pan. Grease lightly with butter. Pour a ladleful of batter, swirl the pan swiftly so as to spread the batter thinly. When underside is cooked turn the pancake and cook on the other side. Remove to a plate.

6. Place the filling in the middle of the pancake, and fold over.

7. Serve with cream.

Quick Tip

Pancakes should be turned only once for even browning.

Apple Crumble

Preparation Time : 10 minutes

Cooking Time : 30 minutes

To serve 6-8

Ingredients

Milkmaid : 1 tin
Apples : 1 kg
Butter : 50 gm

For crumble :
Maida : 150 gm
Butter : 75 gm

Method

1. Preheat oven to 160° C.

2. Mix together butter and Milkmaid and heat for 4 to 5 minutes. Keep aside to cool.

3. Peel and slice apples.

4. In an ovenproof dish, place the apple slices in layers. Press lightly while putting the apple slices. Pour the cooled Milkmaid mixture over it and spread evenly.

5. Mix the *maida*, and butter to a crumbly texture. Top the apples with the crumble.

6. Bake at 160° C for 25 to 30 minutes in a preheated oven.

Apple Custard

Preparation Time : 15-20 minutes

Cooking Time : 45-50 minutes

To serve 8-10

Ingredients

Milkmaid : $^1/_2$ tin
Apple : $^1/_2$ kg
Milk : 1 cup
Eggs : 2

Sugar : 1 tbsp
Nutmeg powder : a pinch
Water : $^1/_4$ cup

Method

1. Chop and stew apples in 1 tbsp sugar and $^1/_4$ cup water (approx 7 to 10 minutes).

2. Cool and blend stewed apples with Milkmaid, milk, beaten eggs and nutmeg powder.

3. Pour into a greased dish and cover with foil or lid.

4. Steam in a pan of hot water for 30 to 40 minutes.

5. Cool. Unmould. Serve hot or chilled.

Apple Crumble

Puddings

Mocha Chip Torte

Striped Coffee Pudding

Lemon Sponge Pudding

Orange Delight

Chocolate Soufflé

Cream Caramel

Cheeseless Cheese Cake

Coffee Pie

Mocha Exquisite

Bread Pudding

Lemon Meringue Pie

Orange Soufflé

Pineapple Soufflé

German Cheese Cake

Biscuit Cake

Floating Island

Mocha Chip Torte

Preparation Time : 15 minutes

Cooking Time : 10 minutes

To serve 8

Ingredients

Milkmaid : $^1/_2$ cup
Milk : 1 cup
Eggs : 2 separated
Pure instant coffee : 1 tbsp
Gelatine : 1 tbsp
Cream : $1^1/_3$ cups
Chocolate : 50 gm chopped (optional)
Walnuts : 50 gm (optional)

Method

1. Beat the egg yolks. Add Milkmaid and milk.

2. Dissolve gelatine in 2 tbsp hot water. Mix in coffee powder.

3. Add to the milk mixture and stir.

4. Stirring constantly, heat the above mixture over a pan of hot water till the mixture becomes thick and creamy. Remove and cool.

5. Beat the cream till light and fluffy. Beat the egg whites to soft peak stage.

6. Fold the beaten cream and egg whites into the cooled custard. Add nuts and chocolate.

7. Chill quickly in the freezer of a refrigerator till well set. Cut and serve.

Quick Tip

The best way to separate egg yolks from egg whites is to crack each egg shell with a knife into two halves. Pull away half of the shell, leaving the yolk in the other half. Gently pass the yolk back and forth between the two halves until all the white has dripped into the bowl.

Mocha Chip Torte

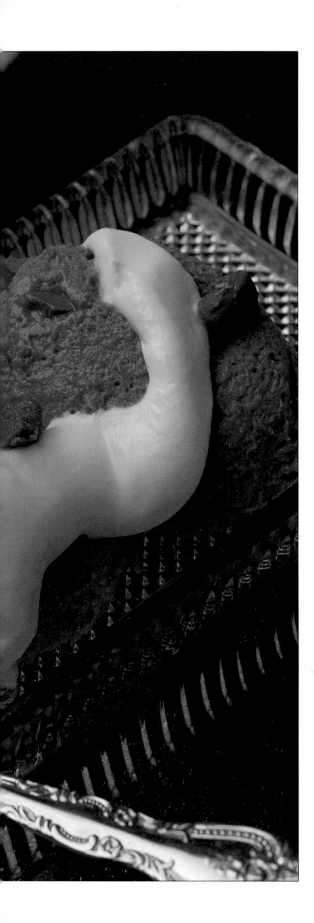

Mocha Exquisite

Preparation Time : 30 minutes

No cooking required

To serve 10-12

Ingredients

Milkmaid : 1 tin
Powdered sugar : 2 tbsp
Unsalted butter : 250 gm
Biscuits : 200 gm
Cream : $1^1/_2$ cups
Egg : 1
Cocoa : 4 tbsp
Coffee : 4 tbsp
Walnuts : $^1/_2$ cup

Method

1. Cream butter and sugar together till light and fluffy.

2. Beat egg well and mix into butter mixture.

3. Add coffee and cocoa. Mix well.

4. Whip cream. Add Milkmaid to it and fold into butter mixture.

5. Crush biscuits and walnuts coarsely. Add to the butter mixture (save 2 tbsp for topping.)

6. Serve frozen, topped with crumbled biscuits and walnuts.

Striped Coffee Pudding

Preparation Time : 5 minutes

Cooking Time : 5 minutes

To serve 10

Ingredients

Milkmaid : $^1/_2$ tin
Water : 4 cups
Pure instant coffee : 8 tsp
Sugar : 4 tbsp
Gelatine : 4 tbsp
Cream : 1 cup
Cherries : (optional)

Method

1. Soak gelatine in 1 cup of water. Dissolve by heating over a pan of hot water or in a double boiler.

2. Dissolve coffee powder in the remaining 3 cups of hot water. Divide the liquor into two equal portions.

3. To one portion add sugar and half the dissolved gelatine. Keep aside this black coffee jelly mixture.

4. To the other portion add Milkmaid and the remaining gelatine. Mix well, to get milk coffee jelly mixture.

5. In small loaf tin pour $^1/_2$" layer of black coffee jelly mixture. Chill until set.

6. Pour $^1/_2$" layer of milk coffee jelly mixture over set coffee jelly mixture and chill till set. Repeat layers until jelly mixtures are used up. Chill until set.

7. Dip loaf tin in hot water to loosen jelly. Invert over a plate to unmould.

8. Whip cream till a little thick but flowing.

9. Cut jelly into thick slices and serve cold with whipped cream.

Quick Tip

Soaking gelatine in cold water for a few minutes before heating helps dissolve the gelatine more uniformly.

Striped Coffee Pudding

Bread Pudding

Preparation Time : 10 minutes

Cooking Time : 40 minutes

To serve 6-8

Ingredients

Milkmaid : $^1/_2$ tin
Bread slices : 6
Milk : 1 cup
Butter : 25 gm
Eggs : 2, beaten
Kishmish : 50 gm
A pinch of nutmeg powder

Method

1. Preset the oven at 160° C. Trim the edges of bread slices.

2. Butter the slices on both sides and cut into two triangular pieces.

3. Arrange the slices in layers in an 8" x 6" oven proof dish, sprinkling the *kishmish* in between the layers.

4. Mix together Milkmaid, milk, eggs and nutmeg and beat lightly. Pour the mixture over the buttered slices.

5. Bake in a moderately hot oven (160° C) for 30 to 40 minutes till the top is golden brown.

6. Serve hot or cold as desired.

Quick Tip

Before actual preparation of a baked dish, check the oven temperature and prepare the baking tin.

Lemon Sponge Pudding

Preparation Time : 10 minutes

Cooking Time : 40-50 minutes

To serve 6

Ingredients

Milkmaid : 1 tin
Eggs : 5, separated
Maida : 50 gm
Butter : 50 gm
Milk : 2 cups
Juice of 4 lemons

Method

1. Preheat the oven to 160° C. Place a dish containing water in the oven. Prepare the baking dish. Grease the pie dish for baking

2. Cream butter. Add lemon juice, egg yolks and Milkmaid. Beat well.

3. Add milk and *maida*. Mix well.

4. Beat the egg whites till stiff. Fold into milk and *maida* mixture. Pour into the greased pie dish.

5. Place baking dish in the dish containing water in the oven.

6. Bake at 160° C for 40 to 50 minutes.

7. Serve hot or chilled.

Lemon Meringue Pie

Preparation Time : 15-20 minutes

Cooking Time : 20 minutes

To serve 6

Ingredients

Milkmaid : 1 tin
Biscuit : 200 gm
Butter : 100 gm
Eggs : 3, separated
Powdered sugar : $^1/_2$ cup
Juice of 6 lemons
Rind of 1 lemon

Method

1. Crush the biscuits to powder. Preset the oven at 160° C. Melt butter.

2. Mix biscuit crumbs with melted butter.

3. Press the mixture onto the base and sides of an 8" pie dish. Chill in refrigerator.

4. In a bowl combine Milkmaid, lemon juice, lemon rind and lightly beaten egg yolks.

5. Spoon the mixture into the chilled crumb crust.

6. Whisk egg whites till stiff, gradually adding powdered sugar. Spoon the meringue onto the filling so as to cover it.

7. Bake in a moderate oven (160° C) for 15 to 20 minutes or till the meringue is golden brown.

8. Serve hot/chilled in refrigerator.

Lemon Meringue Pie

Orange Delight

Preparation Time : 10 minutes

Cooking Time : 5 minutes

To serve 8-10

Ingredients

Milkmaid : 1 tin
Cream : 2 cups
Tinned orange juice : 3 cups
Gelatine : 3 tbsp
Orange : $^1/_2$ (optional)

Method

1. Soak gelatine in orange juice. Heat over a pan of hot water till gelatine dissolves. Cool.

2. Whip cream. (Save 3 to 4 tbsp cream for decorating). Fold in Milkmaid.

3. Mix in juice and gelatine mixture. Pour into a chill tray and freeze.

4. Serve decorated with orange sections or peel and stiffly beaten cream.

Quick Tip

To remove the pith and skin from orange segments use a pair of kitchen scissors instead of a knife.

Orange Delight

Orange Soufflé

Preparation Time : 15 minutes

Cooking Time : 5 minutes

To serve 10-12

Ingredients

Milkmaid : 1 tin
Oranges : 2, rind and juice of $^1/_2$ orange, skinned, chopped segments of $1^1/_2$ oranges
Gelatine : $2^1/_2$ tbsp
Milk : $1^2/_3$ cups
Cream : $1^1/_3$ cups

Method

1▷ Soak gelatine in $^1/_2$ cup water. Dissolve over a pan of hot water.

2▷ Mix the dissolved gelatine with Milkmaid, milk, rind, and juice. Add finely chopped orange segments, saving some for decoration.

3▷ Whip up cream till stiff. Fold into the Milkmaid orange mixture.

4▷ Pour the mixture into a soufflé dish and chill.

5▷ Serve decorated with stiffly beaten cream and glazed cherry or candied peel or orange segments.

Chocolate Soufflé

Preparation Time : 10 minutes

Cooking Time : 5 minutes

To serve 10-12

Ingredients

Milkmaid : 1 tin
Cocoa : 3-4 tbsp
Chocolate : 50 gm
Walnuts : 50 gm chopped
Gelatine : $2^1/_2$ tbsp
Milk : 2 cups
Cream : $1^1/_3$ cup

Method

1▷ Dissolve gelatine in $^1/_2$ cup water over a pan of hot water.

2▷ Add cocoa to 1 cup milk. Heat over a pan of hot water and make a smooth paste.

3▷ Add dissolved gelatine, cocoa paste, rest of milk, chopped walnuts and chocolate pieces to Milkmaid. Mix well.

4▷ Whisk cream till stiff. Fold into the Milkmaid mixture.

5▷ Pour the mixture into a soufflé dish and chill.

6▷ Serve decorated with stiffly beaten cream and chocolate curls.

Pineapple Soufflé

Preparation Time : 15 minutes

Cooking Time : 5 minutes

To serve 10-12

Ingredients

Milkmaid : 1 tin
Tinned pineapple : 3 to 4 slices, chopped
Gelatine : $2^1/_2$ tbsp
Cream : $1^1/_3$ cups
Juice of 4 lemons
Milk : $1^2/_3$ cups

Method

1▷ Soak gelatine in $^1/_2$ cup of water. Dissolve over a pan of hot water.

2▷ Mix the dissolved gelatine with Milkmaid, milk, finely chopped pineapple slices and lemon juice.

3▷ Whip up cream till stiff. Mix into the Milkmaid pineapple mixture.

4▷ Pour the mixture into a soufflé dish and chill in the refrigerator.

5▷ When set, decorate with stiffly beaten cream, glazed cherry or candied peel and serve.

Quick Tip

Tinned pineapple may be substituted with fresh pineapple slices stewed in sugar. Use 1 tbsp sugar and 1 tbsp water for each slice.

Cream Caramel

Cream Caramel

Preparation Time : 5 minutes

Cooking Time : 40 minutes

To serve 8

Ingredients

Milkmaid : 1 tin
Milk : 500 ml
Eggs : 4
Lemon : 1 grated rind only
Sugar : 2 tbsp (to coat the mould with caramelised
sugar)

Method

1. Preset the oven at 180° C. Place a shallow pan of water in the oven.

2. Heat sugar in the ring mould till it melts and caramelises. Turn the mould so as to coat its base and sides with the caramel. Keep aside.

3. Combine Milkmaid and milk together.

4. Beat the eggs lightly. Add lemon rind. Gradually add milk and mix well.

5. Pour into the caramelised ring mould. Place the mould in the pan of water in the oven and bake for 30 to 40 minutes.

6. Cool. Chill in refrigerator for 5 to 6 hours before unmoulding to serve.

German Cheese Cake

Preparation Time : 25-30 minutes

Cooking Time : 1 hour

To serve 8-10

Ingredients

Pastry :

Maida : 250 gm
Cold salted butter : 125 gm
(or salt free butter + $^1/_4$ tsp salt)
Cold water : 6-8 tbsp

Filling :

Milkmaid : $^1/_2$ tin   Paneer : 250 gm
Egg yolks : 4
Lemon : 1 finely grated rind and juice
Ground almonds : 30 gm
Chopped sultanas : 50 gm
Finely chopped candied peel : 50 gm

Meringue :

Egg white : 1   Sugar : 50 gm, powdered

Method

1. Preheat the oven at 180° C.

2. Cut cold butter into small pieces.

3. Using a palette knife rub butter into the *maida*.

4. Sprinkle cold water over *maida* and using a palette knife combine into a ball.

5. With minimum handling, roll into $^1/_8$" thick pastry.

6. Lift the pastry over the rolling pin, drop into pie dish and line it. Trim off the extra dough.

7. Prick the pastry with a fork (to prevent puffing). Bake blind at 180° C for 10 to 15 minutes. Remove from oven.

8. Reset the oven at 140° C.

9. Blend together *paneer*, egg yolks and Milkmaid till smooth and creamy. Add almond powder, sultanas, peel, rind and lemon juice. Mix well. Pour into the baked pastry case. Whisk egg white till stiff. Add half the sugar gradually and continue to whisk till stiff peak stage. Fold in the rest of the sugar and pipe a fine lattice of meringue over the pie.

10. Return to oven and bake at 140° C for 45 minutes or till meringue is crisp. Serve hot or chilled with cream.

Cheeseless Cheese Cake

Preparation Time : 10 minutes

Cooking Time : 40 minutes

To serve 8

Ingredients

Milkmaid : 1 tin
Eggs : 4, separated
Cornflour : $2^1/_2$ tbsp
Juice of 3 lemons
Powdered biscuits : 2 tbsp
Butter : 1 tbsp

Method

1. Preset the oven at 180° C. Grease the baking dish with butter.

2. Beat the egg yolks till creamy. Add Milkmaid, cornflour, and lemon juice one by one, beating well after each addition.

3. Beat the egg white till stiff.

4. Fold the stiffly beaten egg whites into the Milkmaid mixture.

5. Sprinkle the buttered dish with half the crumbled biscuits. Pour in the mixture and sprinkle with the remaining crushed biscuits.

6. Bake at 180° C for 30 to 40 minutes.

7. Serve hot.

Floating Island

Biscuit Cake

Preparation Time : 15-20 minutes

Cooking Time : 3-5 minutes

To serve 10-12

Ingredients

Milkmaid : $^3/_4$ tin
Biscuits : 30
Jam : 3 tbsp

For coffee butter paste :

Milkmaid : $^1/_4$ tin
Cocoa : 50 gm
Butter : 50 gm
Pure instant coffee : 2 tbsp

For coffee liquor :

Water : 1 cup
Pure instant coffee : 2 tsp

Optional for topping :

Cream : $^1/_2$ cup
Walnuts : 8-10

Method

1. Boil water. Add to 2 tsp coffee powder to prepare coffee liquor.

2. Dip half the biscuits into coffee liquor. Arrange them on the base of a glass serving dish and spread jam.

3. Dip the rest of the biscuits in coffee liquor and arrange a second layer in the dish. Cover with $^1/_2$ tin of Milkmaid.

4. Combine Milkmaid, butter, cocoa and coffee powder to make coffee butter paste.

5. Spread a layer of coffee butter paste over the Milkmaid layer. Top with rest of the Milkmaid.

6. Chill and serve topped with cream and walnuts.

Quick Tip

Small quantities of cream may be substituted with home-made malai.

Coffee Pie

Preparation Time : 10 minutes

Cooking Time : 15 minutes

To serve 8

Ingredients

Pastry :

Maida : 200 gm
Cold salted butter : 100 gm
Cold water : 5-6 tbsp

Filling :

Milkmaid : $^1/_2$ tin
Milk : $2^1/_2$ cups
Pure instant coffee : 4 heaped tbsp
Cornflour : 2 heaped tbsp
Cream : $^1/_4$ cup (for decoration)

Method

1. Preset oven at 180° C.

2. Cut cold butter into small pieces. Using a palette knife rub butter into the *maida*.

3. Sprinkle cold water over *maida* and using palette knife combine into a soft ball.

4. With minimum handling, roll into $^1/_8$" thick pastry, $1^1/_2$" bigger on all sides than the base of the pie dish. Lift it over the rolling pin, drop it into pie dish and line it, trim off the excess.

5. Prick the base and sides or bake blind at 180° C for 10 to 15 minutes.

6. Make a paste of cornflour and coffee with a little milk.

7. Heat Milkmaid and rest of the milk together stirring constantly. When it comes to a boil, add cornflour paste and cook till custard is thick.

8. Pour custard into the prepared pie shell. Return to oven for 10 minutes. Cool to room temperature and chill in the refrigerator.

9. Beat the cream till stiff. Pipe a lattice onto the pie. Chill and serve.

Quick Tip

Pastry dough should be handled to a minimum to get best results.

Floating Island

Preparation Time : 5-10 minutes

Cooking Time : 15 minutes

To serve 4

Ingredients

Milkmaid : $^1/_4$ tin
Milk : 2 cups
Egg yolks : 3
Lemon rind : 1 tsp
Vanilla essence : 1 tsp
Egg white : 1
Castor sugar : 1 tbsp

Jam sauce :

Jam : 3 tbsp
Water : 3 tbsp
Mint leaves for decoration

Method

1. Beat egg white until stiff, gradually beating in castor sugar to form a stiff and glossy meringue. Bring milk to simmer in a deep frying pan.

2. Drop tablespoonfuls of meringue into milk. Poach gently for 2 minutes, then turn and poach for a further 2 minutes. Carefully lift meringues from milk with a slotted spoon, drain on absorbent paper, transfer to a plate and chill until needed.

3. Beat egg yolks. Add Milkmaid and lemon rind. Slowly beat in hot milk used to poach meringues. Place bowl over simmering water and cook, stirring constantly until custard begins to thicken. Remove from heat. Cool, stirring now and then. When cold, stir in essence.

4. Pour custard into individual bowls. Top with a meringue. Chill.

5. Make jam sauce by heating together jam and water till it boils. Remove from fire and cool.

6. To serve add a swirl of jam sauce into each bowl of custard. Decorate with a mint leaf.

Quick Tip

Ordinary table sugar can be powdered and used as a substitute for castor sugar.

Frozen Wonders

Kesar Kulfi

Mango Kulfi

Cherry Yoghurt

Honey & Raisin Yoghurt

Mango Yoghurt

Chikoo Ice-Cream

Pista Ice-Cream

Cherry Ice-cream

Ice-Cream Bombe

Vanilla Ice-Cream
with Chocolate Sauce

Watermelon Sorbet

Orange Sorbet

Coconut Sorbet

Kesar Kulfi

Preparation Time : 15-20 minutes plus freezing time

Cooking Time : 10 minutes

To serve 10

Ingredients

Milkmaid : 1 tin
Milk : 4 cups
Khoa : 100 gm
Maida : 1 tbsp
Chopped and blanched almonds : 10-12
Kesar : $\frac{1}{2}$ tsp powdered

Method

1. Mix together Milkmaid, milk, *maida* and *khoa*. Bring to boil, stirring constantly.

2. Reduce heat and cook for 5 minutes, stirring constantly. Remove from fire. Cool.

3. Add almonds and *kesar* dissolved in 1 tsp of water.

4. Fill into kulfi moulds and freeze overnight.

Mango Kulfi

Preparation Time : 15-20 minutes plus freezing time

Cooking Time : 10 minutes

To serve 10

Ingredients

Milkmaid : 1 tin   Milk : 4 cups
Maida : 1 tbsp   Mangoes : 3 (Medium size)

Method

1. Peel mangoes and remove pulp. Mash the pulp well and keep aside.

2. Mix together Milkmaid, milk, *maida*. Bring to a boil stirring constantly. Remove from fire and cool.

3. Mix in mango pulp and pour into kulfi moulds. Freeze overnight.

Quick Tip

To set kulfis and ice-cream into firm blocks, make sure your refrigerator is at its coldest. Defrost it first, then turn the temperature knob to the coldest mark.

Kesar Kulfi

Cherry Yoghurt

Preparation Time : 15-20 minutes

No cooking required

To serve 5-6

Ingredients

Milkmaid : $^1/_2$ tin
Curd : 500 gm
Tinned cherries : 15-20
Gelatine : $1^1/_2$ tbsp
Cherry flavour : 2-3 drops

Method

1. Destone cherries and chop into small pieces.

2. Dissolve gelatine in $^1/_2$ cup hot water.

3. Combine Milkmaid, curd and gelatine. Beat lightly to get a smooth texture.

4. Add chopped cherries and cherry flavour. Leave in a refrigerator to set.

5. Serve well set.

Honey and Raisin Yoghurt

Preparation Time : 15-20 minutes

No cooking required

To serve 5-6

Ingredients

Milkmaid : $^1/_2$ tin
Curd : 500 gm
Honey : 2 tbsp
Raisins : 50 gm (soaked overnight)
Gelatine : $1^1/_2$ tbsp

Method

1. In a bowl combine Milkmaid, curd, and honey. Beat well to break up lumps.

2. Dissolve gelatine in $^1/_2$ cup hot water.

3. Add to the curd mixture and leave to set in a refrigerator.

4. When half set, add the soaked raisins and return to the refrigerator.

5. Serve well set.

Mango Yoghurt

Preparation Time : 15-20 minutes

No cooking required

To serve 5-6

Ingredients

Milkmaid : $^1/_2$ tin
Curd : 500 gm
Mango : 1 (medium size)
Gelatine : $1^1/_2$ tbsp
Water : $^1/_2$ cup

Method

1. Dissolve gelatine in $^1/_2$ cup hot water.

2. Peel mango and slice. Reserve 1 slice for decoration and mash the rest into pulp.

3. Beat the curd lightly to break up the lumps.

4. In a serving bowl combine Milkmaid, curd, mango pulp and dissolved gelatine.

5. Leave in a refrigerator to set.

6. Serve well set decorated with thin slices of mangoes.

Quick Tip

Sprinkling a little salt and water in the freezer helps lower the temperature further.

Mango Yoghurt

Chikoo Ice-Cream

Preparation Time : 15-20 minutes plus freezing time

No cooking required

To serve 5-6

Ingredients

Milkmaid : 1 tin
Cold milk : $1^1/_2$ cup
Cream : 3 cups
Chikoo : $^1/_2$ kg

Method

1. Peel *chikoos*. Remove stones and mash well in a blender. Keep aside.

2. Combine Milkmaid, milk and cream. Freeze till the mixture starts freezing at the edges.

3. Remove from freezer and beat until smooth.

4. Add *chikoo* pulp. Mix well and return to the freezer.

5. Freeze till firm.

Pista Ice-Cream

Preparation Time : 15-20 minutes

No cooking required

To serve 5-6

Ingredients

Milkmaid : 1 tin
Cold milk : $1^1/_2$ cup
Cream : 3 cups
Powdered pista : 1 tbsp
Almond essence : $^1/_2$ tsp

Method

1. Combine Milkmaid, milk and cream in a bowl.

2. Add almond essence and powdered *pista*. Mix well.

3. Pour into freezing trays and freeze till the mixture is half set.

4. Remove from the freezer and beat until smooth.

5. Return to freezer and set until firm.

Cherry Ice-Cream

Preparation Time : 15-20 minutes

No cooking required

To serve 5-6

Ingredients

Milkmaid : 1 tin
Cold milk : $1^1/_2$ cup
Cream : 3 cups
Cherry pulp : 1 cup
Pink food colour : $^1/_2$ tsp

Method

1. Combine Milkmaid, milk, cream, cherry pulp and food colour. Blend well.

2. Pour into freezing trays and freeze till the mixture is half set.

3. Remove from freezer. Whisk till smooth.

4. Refreeze till firm.

Ice-Cream Bombe

Preparation Time : 25-30 minutes plus freezing time

No cooking required

To serve 6-8

Ingredients

Milkmaid Cherry Ice-Cream : 2 cups
Milkmaid Pista Ice-Cream : 2 cups
Chopped cashewnuts and pistas : 1 cup
Cake slices : 4-5
Whipped cream : $^1/_2$ cup
Chopped fruit peel : 2 tbsp

Method

1. Line the bottom of a cake tin with chopped nuts.

2. Cover with *pista* ice-cream and freeze till firm.

3. Cover the *pista* ice-cream with cherry ice-cream and freeze again.

4. Press cake slices over the ice-cream. Unmould so that cake forms the base of ice-cream bombe.

5. Decorate and serve with cream and fruit peel.

Cherry Ice-Cream

98

Vanilla Ice-Cream with Chocolate Sauce

Preparation Time : 25-30 minutes plus freezing time

No cooking required

To serve 5-6

Ingredients

Ice-cream :

Milkmaid : $^3/_4$ tin
Cold milk : $1^1/_2$ cup
Cream : $1^1/_2$ cup
Vanilla essence : 1 tsp

Chocolate sauce :

Milkmaid : $^1/_4$ tin
Milk : $^1/_2$ cup
Cocoa : 3 tbsp
Unsalted butter : 50 gm

Method

Ice-cream :

1. Combine the Milkmaid, milk and vanilla essence in a bowl.

2. Whip up the cream lightly and fold into the above mixture.

3. Pour the mixture into a freezing tray and freeze till the mixture is half set.

4. Remove from freezer and beat until smooth.

5. Return to tray and freeze until firm.

Chocolate sauce :

1. Combine milk and cocoa and stir to paste.

2. Add Milkmaid and unsalted butter. Heat over medium flame till thick enough and glossy.

3. Serve ice-cream with hot chocolate sauce.

Quick Tips

To prevent ice-crystals forming in the ice-cream, cover the container. You must also beat up the half set ice-cream.

Your mixture freezes better in an aluminium or thin bottomed metal container.

Watermelon Sorbet (Facing page)
Vanilla Ice-Cream with Chocolate Sauce

Watermelon Sorbet

Preparation Time : 10-15 minutes plus freezing time

No cooking required

To serve 6-8

Ingredients

Milkmaid : $^1/_2$ tin
Watermelon pulp : $^1/_2$ kg

Method

 Remove all seeds from the watermelon and cut into small pieces.

 Mix in Milkmaid and blend in an electric blender. Pour into freezing trays and freeze till set. Cut into cubes and serve frozen.

Orange Sorbet

Preparation Time : 5 minutes plus freezing time

No cooking required

To serve 6-8

Ingredients

Milkmaid : $^1/_2$ tin   Orange juice : 4 cups

Method

 Combine Milkmaid and orange juice.

 Pour into freezer trays and freeze till set. Cut into cubes and serve frozen.

Coconut Sorbet

Preparation Time : 20-25 minutes plus freezing time

No cooking required

To serve 6-8

Ingredients

Milkmaid : $^1/_2$ tin   Water : 4 cups
Coconut : 1

Method

 Grate coconut. Add 4 cups of hot water and keep for 15 minutes. Strain through muslin cloth to squeeze out coconut milk.

 Combine Milkmaid with coconut milk and mix well. Pour the mixture into freezing trays and freeze till set. Cut into cubes and serve frozen.

Coconut Sorbet

Children's Party Time

Coconut Mice

Sweet Bread Rolls

Jelly Cards

Tropical Freeze

Traffic Lights

Jelly Slices

Chocolate Biscuits

Milky Jujubes

Marzipan

Ice-Cream Soda

Coconut Mice

Preparation Time : 15-20 minutes

No cooking required

To serve 10-12

Ingredients

Milkmaid : $^1/_2$ tin
Desiccated coconut powder : 200 gm
Icing sugar : 100 gm
Almonds : 8-10, cut into slivers for ears
Glazed cherries : 4-5 cut into small pieces for
noses
Silver balls : 10-15 for eyes.

Method

1. Mix together Milkmaid, desiccated coconut powder and icing sugar to get a soft dough.

2. Take a small quantity of dough, the size of a lemon and form into an elongated mouse shape.

3. Use silver balls for eyes, glazed cherry pieces for noses and almond silvers for ears.

4. Leave in a cool place.

Quick Tip

For making almond slivers, soak almonds in hot water for 5 minutes and then cut with a sharp knife.

Coconut Mice

106

Sweet Bread Rolls

Preparation Time : 10 minutes

Cooking Time : 15 minutes

To serve 8

Ingredients

Milkmaid : $^1/_3$ tin
Assorted dry fruit : $^1/_2$ cup chopped
Elaichi : 2-3
Slices of bread : 8
Ghee : 1 tsp
Oil for frying

Method

1. Heat 1 tsp *ghee*. Add Milkmaid, chopped nuts and powdered *elaichi*. Cook over low flame till the mixture becomes dry and leaves the sides of the pan.

2. Cut the sides of the bread slices.

3. Dip the bread slices in water one at a time, squeeze out water by pressing the flat whole slices between the palms of the hands.

4. Place some filling in the middle of the slice. Roll and press into shape. Deep fry in fat till golden brown.

5. Drain on absorbent paper and serve hot.

Jelly Cards

Preparation Time : 10-15 minutes

Cooking Time : 5 minutes

To serve 12

Ingredients

Milkmaid : 1 tin
Orange jelly crystals : 100 gm
Lemon jelly crystals : 100 gm

Method

1. Dissolve orange jelly crystals in 400 ml water. Add $^1/_2$ tin Milkmaid and mix well.

2. Pour to $^1/_4$" thickness in a flat dish and leave to set in freezer.

3. Dissolve lemon jelly crystals in 400 ml water. Add $^1/_2$ tin Milkmaid and mix well.

4. Pour to $^1/_2$" thickness in another flat dish and leave to set in the freezer.

5. When set, cut lemon jelly into rectangular pieces similar to playing cards and keep aside.

6. Cut the orange jelly into small hearts, spades, diamonds, etc. and place on top of the yellow jelly cards.

7. Chop the remaining orange jelly into small pieces and spread on the base of the serving dish. Place the cards on top of the orange jelly.

8. Keep refrigerated till served.

Tropical Freeze

Preparation Time : 15-20 minutes

No cooking required

To serve 6

Ingredients

Milkmaid : 1 cup
Coconut milk (thick) : 1 cup
Egg yolks : 2
Cream : 1 cup
Gelatine : 1 tbsp
Vanilla essence : 1 tsp
Orange colour : Few drops
Mango : 1 (medium size), diced.

Method

1. Set refrigerator control at coldest point.

2. Soak gelatine in 2 tbsp water for 5 minutes in a bowl.

3. Place the bowl in a shallow pan containing hot water.

4. Stir the gelatine till it dissolves.

5. In a mixing bowl, whisk cream till thick and fluffy. Whisk in Milkmaid, egg yolk, gelatine, coconut milk and essence. Add colour.

6. Freeze in ice-trays, until almost firm.

7. Remove from freezer. Beat well and refreeze until firm.

8. Serve decorated with mango pieces.

Variation :

Raspberry red colour and cherries may be used instead of orange colour and mango.

Traffic Lights

Preparation Time : 10-15 minutes

Cooking Time : 10-12 minutes

Makes 24 bars

Ingredients

Milkmaid : 1 tin
Butter : 100 gm
Cocoa powder : 6 tbsp
Biscuits : 200 gm
Red, green and yellow candied fruit for lights.

Method

1. In a pan, combine Milkmaid, cocoa powder and butter. Heat with constant stirring.

2. When the mixture starts bubbling at the sides, reduce flame and cook on medium heat for 8 to 10 minutes.

3. Mix in the coarsely broken biscuits and remove from fire.

4. Spread mixture onto a greased plate and leave to cool.

5. When cool, cut into $2\frac{1}{2}$"-3" bars and decorate with small rounds of three different coloured candied fruit.

Traffic Lights

Jelly Slices

Jelly Slices

Preparation Time : 15-20 minutes

Cooking Time : 5 minutes

To serve 12

Ingredients

Milkmaid : 1 tin
Butter : 100 gm
Biscuits : 200 gm
Jelly : (preferably red in colour) 100 gm
Gelatine : 1 tbsp
Lemon juice : 1 tbsp
Cream : $^1/_4$ cup (optional)
Chopped nuts : 2 tbsp (optional)

Method

1st layer :

1. Crush biscuits

2. Melt butter and mix in biscuit crumbs.

3. Press the mixture into the base of a rectangular tin. Freeze for 20 minutes.

2nd layer :

1. Dissolve gelatine in $^1/_2$ cup of hot water. Pour in Milkmaid and add lemon juice.

2. Pour this over biscuit layer and cool till gelatine is set.

3rd layer :

1. Dissolve jelly crystals in 450 ml of hot water. Cool. Pour over 2nd layer.

2. Freeze till set.

3. Cut into pieces. Top with whipped cream and/or chopped nuts and serve.

111

Chocolate Biscuits

Chocolate Biscuits

Preparation Time : 15 minutes

Cooking Time : 10 minutes

To serve 8

Ingredients

Milkmaid : $^1/_2$ tin
Butter : 50 gm
Cocoa powder : $1^1/_2$ tbsp
Biscuits : 16
Cashewnuts : 10, halved
Coconut powder : $^1/_2$ cup
Green and yellow colours
Small rounds of coloured candied fruit for eyes

Method

1> Heat Milkmaid, cocoa powder and butter in a pan. Cook till the mixture starts leaving the sides of the pan. Remove from fire.

2> Spread 1 tsp of this mixture onto each biscuit and leave to dry for 5 minutes.

3> Divide the coconut powder into 2 portions. Colour one green and the other yellow.

4> Decorate each biscuit by making eyes with candied fruit, mouth with cashew halves and hair with coloured coconut powder.

Milky Jujubes

Preparation Time : 5 minutes plus overnight setting time

Cooking Time : 15-20 minutes

To serve 12-15

Ingredients

Milkmaid : 1 tin
Sugar : 500 gm
Water : $2^1/_2$ cup
Gelatine : 75 gm
Citric acid : 1 tsp
Powdered sugar : 1 cup to coat jujubes
Colours and flavours

Method

1> Soak gelatine in $1^1/_2$ cup water.

2> In a pan put together the remaining water, sugar and citric acid and bring to boil.

3> Add the soaked gelatine and heat on medium fire till gelatine is dissolved.

4> Remove from fire. Add in Milkmaid and stir. Divide into 2 to 3 portions. Colour and flavour each portion differently.

5> Pour into greased trays and set overnight.

6> Loosen the set gelatine from the tray. Spread powdered sugar on a sheet of paper and turn out the set gelatine onto it.

7> Cut into squares and coat each piece with sugar just before serving.

Quick Tips

Whenever colours and flavourings are used, they should be put in after the cooking process unless otherwise specified.

Juice of 1 to 2 lemons may be used if citric acid is not available.

Marzipan

Marzipan

Preparation Time : 10-15 minutes

No cooking required

To serve 10

Ingredients

Milkmaid : $^1/_2$ tin
Cashewnuts : 250 gm, powdered fine
Icing sugar : 1 cup
Almond essence : $^1/_2$ tsp
Colours : red, yellow and green

Method

1 > In a bowl combine the sugar, cashewnut powder and essence.

2 > Add Milkmaid in small quantities to make a firm but pliable dough. Knead the dough till smooth.

3 > Divide into portions. Colour, flavour and shape as desired.

Ice-Cream Soda

Preparation Time : 5 minutes

No cooking required

To serve 8

Ingredients

Milkmaid : 1 tin
Lemon essence : 1 tsp
Green colour : $^1/_4$ tsp
Aerated soda : 8 bottles, chilled
Cream : 8 tbsp

Method

1. Whip cream till it forms soft peaks. Keep aside.

2. Mix Milkmaid with lemon essence and green colour. Divide equally into 8 tall glasses.

3. In each glass pour $^1/_3$ of the bottle of chilled soda and mix well.

4. Add 1 tbsp of whipped cream to each glass and pour the remaining soda to fill the glasses.

5. Serve immediately.

Variation

For Strawberry Ice-Cream Soda, use strawberry essence and raspberry red colour.

Ice-Cream Soda

Culinary Equipment

Mixing Tools

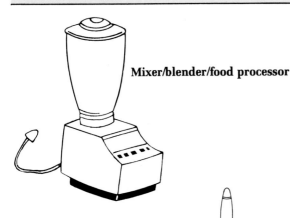

Mixer/blender/food processor

Spring egg beater. A hand-operated kitchen tool used for beating, stirring or whipping.

Wire balloon whisk. It is used for beating eggs, stirring sauces and whipping creams.

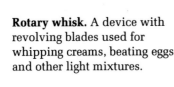

Rotary whisk. A device with revolving blades used for whipping creams, beating eggs and other light mixtures.

Spoons and Spatulas

Cutting tools. A basic collection of cutting tools is vital in any well-equipped kitchen. Store sharp knives separately from other cutlery, so that the edges do not become dulled or damaged. A slotted rack in the drawer or a magnetic rack hung on the wall are ideal.

Kitchen scissors

Ladle

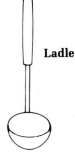

Wooden Spatula. A flat, thin wooden implement used for spreading, and mixing substances.

Slotted spoon. A metal spoon with slits used for frying purposes.

Perforated spoon. A flat metal spoon with holes used for all types of frying.

Fish slice. A flat metal spoon with shallow slits used for frying of fish.

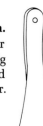

Wooden spoon. A deep wooden spoon used for mixing purposes.

Rubber spatula. A flexible, flat rubber spatula used for scooping purposes. Normally sold as an attachment to mixer.

Pots and Pans.

Good pans should conduct heat evenly, the diameter of the pan should be similar to that of the hot plate or burner in use. The inside of the pan should be smooth with the corners rounded.

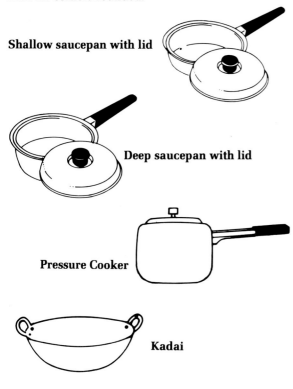

Shallow saucepan with lid

Deep saucepan with lid

Pressure Cooker

Kadai

Knives

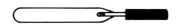

Palette knife. A flat bakery knife, blunt on both edges, used for mixing ingredients like flour, eggs etc.

Ordinary kitchen knife

Bread knife

Serrated knife. This knife is useful for slicing citrus fruits.

Baking and Freezing.

A selection of basic shapes and sizes of tins and trays will serve for most cakes and breads, but a few unusually shaped tins will help make your baking more attractive. Most tins are made of alminium as it is a good conductor of heat and cooks evenly.

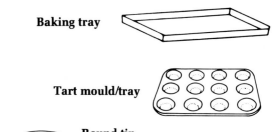

Baking tray

Tart mould/tray

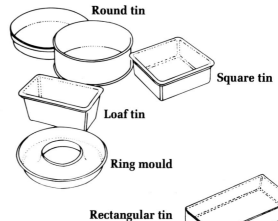

Round tin

Square tin

Loaf tin

Ring mould

Rectangular tin

Pie dish. This is usually made of aluminium, oven proof glass or earthenware.

Wire racks. These are used for cooling freshly baked cakes and biscuits.

Soufflé dish. Porcelain dish used for hot and cold puddings.

Jelly mould. Ridged aluminium round tin used to set jellies and puddings.

Ramekins. Small moulds used for baking small decorative cakes.

Kitchen Aids

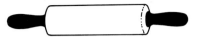

Rolling pin

Sieve

Can-opener

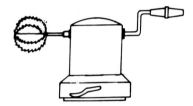

Coconut grater

Potato masher

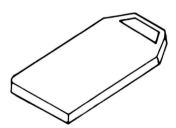

Chopping board

Tongs

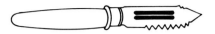

Peeler

Biscuit cutter. A device used to cut pastry, biscuits, doughnuts and confectionary in various shapes.

Pastry cutter. It is used for cutting dough to give it a decorative edge.

Corer-cum-slicer. A very sharp device which slices, simultaneously removing the central core of seeds of various fruits eg. apples.

Icing bag and nozzles. A device used for piping out different shapes and sizes of icing or dough for decorative purposes.

1 Milkmaid tin holds 400 gm Sweetened Condensed Milk.
1 Milkmaid tin = 300 ml
1 tea cup = 150 ml = $^1/_2$ Milkmaid tin = 15 tbsp
1 tbsp = 10 ml = 2 tsp*
1 tsp = 5 ml = $^1/_2$ tbsp**
*tsp = teaspoon
**tbsp = tablespoon

All measures are level measures unless mentioned otherwise.
All cup measures are till the goldline marking in the household tea cup.

Ingredients	Cup Measures A 150 ml cup holds :
Rice/dals	150 gm
Besan	80 gm
Atta/maida	100 gm
Suji	120 gm
Sugar	175 gm
Cocoa	50 gm
Cornflour	80 gm
Bread/Biscuit crumbs	100 gm/60 gm
Kaju powder	80 gm
Coconut powder	50 gm
Full cream milk powder	80 gm
Cream	150 gm
Cooking oil	150 gm
Melted ghee	150 gm
Melted butter	150 gm
Milk	180 gm
Honey	240 gm

GLOSSARY OF INGREDIENTS

Usage In Book	Assamese	Bengali	Gujarati
Almonds	Badam	Badam	Badam
Apricots	Malhoi	Khubani fal	Jardalu
Besan (Gram flour)	Basan	Besan	Vesan or chana-no lot
Black Cardamom	Dangor elachi	Baro elach	Kali elchi Or Moti elchi
Candied peel	Mitha bakoli	Misti khosa faler	Khand ma bolela fal
Cashewnuts	Kaju	Kaju badam	Kaju
Channa (Chick-pea)	Chana	Chana	Chana
Cherries	Cherry	Cherries	Cherries
Chikoo (Sapota)	Chikoo	Safeda	Chikoo
Cinnamon	Dalchini	Daruchini	Taj
Coconut	Narikol	Narikel	Nalier koprun
Curd (Yoghurt)	Doi	Dadhi	Dahin
Desiccated coconut powder	Shukan narikol goori	Sukno Narikel guro	Kopara chhin
Edible camphor	Khoa karpur	Khabar karpur	Khawa-nun kapoor
Elaichi (Cardamom)	Soru elachi	Choto elach	Lili elchi or nani elchi
Glazed cherries	Taza cherry	Taja cherry	Taji cherries
Guava	Modhuri	Payara	Jamrukh
Honey	Mow	Madhu	Madh
Kesar (Saffron whole)	Zafrang	Kesar	Kesar
Kesari powder (Saffron powder)	Zafrang goori	Kesri powder	Kesari powder
Khoa (Dried milk solids)	Khoya	Khoa	Mavo or mava

Hindi	Kannada	Marathi	Malayalam	Oriya	Tamil	Telugu
Badam	Baadami	Badam	Badam	Badam	Badam paruppu	Baadam
Khubani	Apricot	Jardaloo	Apricot	Khubani badam	Apricot	Apricot pandlu
Besan	Besan or kadali hittu	Besan	Kadala mavu	Besan	Kadalai maavu	Sanaga pindi
Badi elaychi	Kari aelakki	Masalyachi velchi	Valiya elakkai	Alaicha	Peria yelakkai	Pedda yelakulu
Paga hua chilka	Sakkare paakadalli hakitt sippe	Pakat Gho lawalelye Saali	Panchasara-ppavil/ Uppil vazhattiya	Sharkarita chali	Sarkarayil ooravaitha tholi	Naanabettina pandla thokkalu
Kaju	Godambi	Kajoo	Andiparippu	Kaju badam	Mundiri paruppu	Jedipappu
Channa	Kadali bele	Chana	Kadala	Channa	Kadalai (or) kondai kadalai	Sanagalu
Cherries	Cherry	Cherries	Cherry pazham	Cherry phala	Cherry pazham	Cherry pandlu
chikoo	Sapota	Chikkoo	Sappotta	Sapeta	Sappotta pazham	Sappota pandlu
Dal cheenee	Dal chinni	Dalchini	Karuka patta	Dalchini	Elavanga pattai	Dalchi-nachekka
Nariyal	Tengu	Naral	Thenga	Nadiaa	Thengai	Kobbarikaya
Dahi	Mosaru	Dahi	Thairu	Dahi	Thayir	Perugu
Sukha nari-yal powder	Ona kubbari pudi	Sukya khobaryacha Chura	Kopra podi	Khuruda Nadia chura	Ularndha thengai podi	Kobbari koru
Khane ka kapoor	Tinnuva karpoora	Khayacha Kapur	Pacha kar-pooram	Khaibajogya Karpura	Pachhai kar-pooram	Pachhakar-pooram
Choti elayachi	Hasiru aelakki	Lahan Velchi	Elakkai	Gujarati	Yelakkai	Yelakulu
Chikni cherries	Ganjigattida cherry	Tajya cherries	Vilayicha cherry pazham	Chakachakia Cherry phala	Pudhiya Cherry pazham	Poota-poosina cherrylu
Amrood	Seebe hannu	Peroo	Perakkai	Pijuli	Koyya pazham	Jaama pandlu
Shahad	Jenu	Madh	Thean	Mahu	Thean	Tene
Kesar	Kesari	Keshar	Kesari	Kesar	Kumkum-appoo	Kumkuma-ppuvu
Kesari powder	Kesari pudi	Keshari rang	Kesari powder	Kesari Gunda	Kumkuma-poo podi	Kukumapuvvu podum
Khoa	Khoa	Khava	Khoa	Khua	Paledu	Kovaa

GLOSSARY OF INGREDIENTS

Usage In Book	Assamese	Bengali	Gujarati
Leechi	Lechu	Leechu	Leechi
Lemon	Nemu	Lebu	Limbu
Lime	Nemu	Batapi lebu	Lime
Maida (Refined flour)	Maida	Maida	Mendo or menda
Moong dal (Green gram)	Mogu dail	Mug dal	Mag-ni dal
Nutmeg	Jaiphal	Jaifal	Jayfal
Orange	Kamala	Kamola lebu	Santarun
Paneer (Cottage cheese)	Paneer	Chana	Paneer
Pineapple	Anarash	Anaras	Ananas
Raisins	Khissmiss	Kismis	Kismis
Saunf (Anise seeds)	Sof	Mauri	Variyali
Seviyan (Vermecelli)	Sewoin	Semai	Sevi
Silver balls	Roopali gooti	Rupor dana	Chandi-na varakh-ni goli-o
Silver foil or (Vark)	Roopali pat	Rangta	Chandi-no varakh
Suji (Semolina)	Suji	Suji	Soji
Sultanas	Sultana	Monakka	Sultanos
Tutti frooti	Tutti frooti	Tutti frooti	Tutti frooti
Walnuts	Akhrout	Akhrot	Akhrot
Wheat flour	Atta	Gamer atta	Ghaun-no lot
Whole milk powder	Goori gakheer	Cream yukta guro dudh	Sampurna dudh-no powder

Hindi	Kannada	Marathi	Malayalam	Oriya	Tamil	Telugu
Leechi	Leechi	Leechi	Leechi	Lichu	Leechi Pazham	Leechi
Neebu	Gaz nimbe	Limbu	Cheru narangi	Lembu	Yelumichai	Nimma pandu
Khatta neebu	Nimbe hannu	Limbu	Narangi	Jambir	Yelumichai	Nimma pandu
Maida	Maida	Maida	Maida	Maida	Maida maavu	Maida
Moong dal	Hesaru bele	Mugachi dal	Cherupayar parippu	Muga dali	Paasi payaru	Pesarapappu
Jayphal	Jaekai	Jayaphal	Jathikka	Jaiphala	Jhadhikkai	Jaagikaaya
Santara	Kittale hannu	Santre	Orange	Kamala (Santara)	Oranju	Nararinza Pandu
Paneer	Paneer or odeda halina ginna	Paneer	Paalkatti	Chena	Paalaadai Katti	Anasapandu
Annanas	Ananas	Ananas	Kaithachakka	Sapuree	Annasi pazham	Yendud-raksha
Munakka	Ona drakshi	Bedane	Unakka munthiri	Kismis	Ularndha thiratchai	Somp
Saunf	Saunf	Badishop	Perumjee-rakam	Panamahuri	Soambu	
Seviyan	Shaavige	Shevaya	Semiya	Simenin	Semia	Semya
Chandi ki goliyan	Belli goligalu or Bangadi goligalu	Silver balls	Silver balls	Rajata golaka	Velli urundai	Muchhap-oosalu
Chandi ka vark	Belli haale or Bengadi haale	Varkha	Silver foil	Rajata pabak	Velli charugu	Muchhareku
Suji	Rave	Rawa	Rava	Suji	Ravai	Godhumar-avva
Kishmish	Beejavillada drakshi	Manuka	Kuruvillatha mundiringa	Manji kadha badakismis	Vidhai illadha Ularndha Thiratchai	Ginjaleni drakha
Tutti frooti	Hannina mithai	Tuti fruiti	Tutti frooti	Tutti frooti	Tutti frooti	Tutti fruitee
Akhrot	Akrodu	Akrod	Akrod	Akhrot	Akrot	Akrotu
Gehun ka atta	godhi hittu	Kaneek	Gotambu mavu	Gahama atta	Ghodhumai maavu	Godhumap-indi
Malaidar Dudh ka powder	Gatti hallina pudi	Whole milk powder	Pada neekkatha paalpodi	Sampurna swasthyakara gunda dudha	Paalaadai Padiyum Paal podi	Vennapaala podi

Glossary of Cooking Terms

A

Agitate: To keep in motion, stir, shake.

B

Bake. To cook in the oven by dry heat.

Bake blind. The procedure of baking unfilled pastry case. The pastry is weighed down with dry peas or beans on grease-proof paper or pricked to prevent puffing. eg. flans, tarts, etc.

Batter. A mixture of flour, liquid and sometimes other ingredients, of a thin, creamy and pouring consistency.

Beat. To agitate an ingredient or mixture vigorously with a fork, spoon, whisk or electric mixer.

Bind. To add a liquid, egg or melted fat to a dry mixture to hold it together, as in dough making.

Blanch. To treat food with boiling water in order to whiten it, preserve its natural colour, loosen the skin or remove a flavour which is too strong.

Blanch, almonds. Place almonds in cold water and bring to boil slowly. Remove from hot water and plunge into cold water. The skin will loosen up and come off on rubbing.

Blend. To mix together thoroughly two or more ingredients either manually with a spoon or with an electric blender (mixer).

Bombe. A dessert of frozen mixtures arranged and frozen in a mould.

C

Caramel. Dry heating of sugar till it melts and turns to rich brown coloured syrup. On cooling, the syrup solidifies to a transparent, shiny, brittle candy, called caramel.

Caramelise. To heat sugar to a temperature at which it melts to brown substance (caramel).

Chill. To cool food, without freezing, in the refrigerator.

Chop. To cut food into small pieces with a knife or food processor.

Coat. 1. To cover food that is to be fried, with egg and flour or breadcrumbs.

2. To cover cooked food with a thin layer of sauce, mayonnaise or dry powder like coconut.

Coating consistency. The consistency required in a sauce for coating. Test by stirring the sauce and holding the spoon upside down; when the consistency is correct the sauce should coat the back of the spoon.

Combine. To mix or blend together two or more ingredients.

Cream. A term used for making a mixture of fat and sugar creamy (by incorporating air, breaking down the sugar crystals and softening the fat). This is done by working the ingredients against the sides of the mixing bowl using a wooden spoon, hand mixer or a whisk.

Crumbs. Small pieces of fresh bread, stale bread, or biscuits.

Crumb-crust. A casing made with powdered biscuits and melted butter. The mixture is pressed along the sides and base of a flan tin and allowed to set by chilling.

Cut in. A method of combining solid fat with maida as in pastry making. Use a pastry blender or two knives in a cutting motion to break the fat into small pieces - and mix throughout the maida.

D

Deep frying. Sufficient fat is used to cover the food completely. The pan used must be deep enough to be only half full of fat before the food is added.

Dough. A thick mixture of uncooked flour and liquid, often combined with other ingredients; thick enough to knead and roll.

Dredge. To sprinkle food thickly or liberally and evenly with maida, sugar, etc.

Dropping consistency. The consistency of some cake and pudding mixtures before cooking; if a spoonful of mixture is lifted from the basin, and the spoon tilted, it should drop off the spoon in 5 seconds.

Dust. To sprinkle lightly with maida, sugar, spices or seasonings.

F

Fold in. To combine a light, whisked or creamed mixture with other ingredients so that it retains its lightness. Usually done with a wooden spoon or rubber spatula, using an under and over motion, until they are thoroughly mixed.

Fold over. Lift from one side and turn so as to double over itself.

Freeze. To preserve food by deep refrigeration and storage at a temperature of 0° C (32° F) or below.

Fry. To cook in hot fat or oil.

Shallow frying. Only a small quantity of fat is used, in a shallow pan. The food must be turned halfway through to cook both sides.

G

Garnish. An edible decoration added to a savoury to improve the appearance.

Grate. To rub food on grater to produce fine shreds.

Grease. To coat the surface of a dish or tin with fat to prevent sticking of food.

I

Icing. A decorative sugar mixture used to coat cakes and pastries.

K

Knead. To work a dough by hand or machine until soft, smooth and pliable.

L

Lukewarm. Just above body temperature, at about 38° C (100° F).

M

Mash. To beat or crush food to a soft, pulpy stage.

Meringue. Egg white whisked until stiff, may be mixed with sugar and baked until crisp.

Mocha. A blend of chocolate and coffee.

Mould. Container in which a food mixture is set to a definite shape.

P

Pipe. To force a soft mixture through a nozzle, to give a decorative effect; used for icings, whipped cream, creamed potato, meringues, etc.

Poach. To cook in an open pan in simmering liquid.

Purée. Food that has been pressed through a fine sieve or food mill, or blender or food processor, to a smooth thick mixture.

R

Rind. Peel of a fruit, usually lemon or orange.

Rub in. To incorporate fat uniformly into flour using the fingertips; used mainly for short crust pastry.

S

Scald. To heat a liquid, usually milk, to just below boiling point.

Shred. To slice food into very thin, long pieces; a knife or coarse grater is usually used.

Sieve. To rub or press a moist food, such as cooked vegetables or fruit, through a sieve.

Sift. To shake a dry ingredient through a sieve or flour sifter, to remove lumps.

Simmer. To cook in liquid at a temperature just below boiling point, approximately 90° C (205°

F). The liquid should be brought to boil first, then the flame adjusted so that the surface of the liquid just shivers.

Slivers. Long thin segments of fruits or vegetables eg. almond, and mango used for garnishing.

Steam. To cook in steam from rapidly boiling water; a special steaming pan, or an ordinary saucepan with a second container inside may be used. The food should not come into contact with the water.

Stew. To cook slowly, and for a long period, in plenty of simmering liquid. The cooking liquid may be thickened and is served with the finished dish.

Stir. To mix with a circular action, usually with a spoon, fork or spatula.

Strain. To separate liquid from solids, using a sieve, colander, cloth, etc.

Swirl. Whipped up cream or meringue mixture poured lightly over surface in a circle.

Syrup. A concentrated solution of sugar in water. (Golden syrup is a by-product of sugar refining).

T

Torte. Rich, decorative, cake-type dessert, of German origin.

Toss. 1. To stir and mix foods lightly with a lifting motion, using two spoons or forks.

2. To turn quickly by throwing up and catching the food into the pan, as for cooking pancakes.

U

Unmould. To remove from a mould. To unmould aspics and other gelatinized dishes, run the blade of a sharp, thin knife around the inner edges of the mould. Dip the bottom of the mould into hot water for 2 or 3 seconds, cover the top of the mould with a chilled plate, and invert the mould onto the plate. Holding plate and mould together, tap the plate on the table to loosen the contents, which should then slide out onto the plate. If the contents stick, rub the mould gently with a hot, damp towel, or turn the mould and plate over and repeat the entire process.

W

Whip. To beat rapidly, to introduce air into a mixture; usually of cream.

Whisk. To beat rapidly to introduce air into a light mixture using a fork, whisk or a hand mixer, as for cream or egg.

Index